Vegan Under Pressure

New Delicious Recipes to Your Life. Using a Traditional or Electric Pressure Cooker & Simple Plant-Based Diet

Great World Press

V1/03

Table of Contents

Introduction

Veganism is a conscious lifestyle choice. People who are unfamiliar with veganism often do not fully understand the implications of your choice and the impact it has on every aspect of your life. It can be difficult at times, and the goal of this book is to lend a helping hand to make food preparation less time consuming, more fun, and free up your time for other pursuits. A traditional or an electric pressure cooker, also called the Instant Pot, not only means less cooking time, it's a multiple-use kitchen appliance with the potential to create vegan dishes for every meal and occasion. The electric pressure cooker performs the tasks of several other standalone appliances, making it even more versatile.

There is so much misinformation out there about the traditional pressure cooker and the electric pressure cooker, and people love retelling horror stories. This can be off putting and make you doubt whether it really is worth your while to get a pressure cooker.

You must choose a pressure cooker that fulfills your specific needs. That depends on the number of people you regularly cook for, plus whether you want standard pressure cooking operations or prefer the advanced technology that comes with an electric pressure cooker

You must take the time to learn how to operate your pressure cooker, studying the manuals and operating guide provided when you purchase it.

Once you understand how to operate your pressure cooker, it is best to study pressure cooker recipes as there are steps to follow when using a pressure cooker that does not apply to stovetop cooking.

Fundamental differences are the ratios of liquid you must use and the reasons to never overfill your pressure cooker. It is important to do this correctly to ensure your food turns out the way it should with no food disasters. Another important difference is when you should season the food and when you should add thickeners, as this is different from other cooking methods.

Pressure cookers change how you cook, and it brings many incredible benefits that most people don't actually think about. You are able to cook much quicker than on a stovetop, and it is a great energy saver on gas and electricity. Instead of using multiple kitchen appliances, you do it on in one pot. One appliance cooking brings far-reaching convenience of not having far less to clean up, plus a financial saving as you do not have to invest in several kitchen appliances. Your pressure cooker, with its many accessories takes care of everything.

Pressure cookers bring several health benefits as bacteria do not easily survive pressure cooking. This fact is especially helpful for high altitude cooking where the boiling point of water is lower, and bacteria survive easier. People who have stomach and intestinal illnesses benefit as food prepared in a pressure cooker is easier digestible than food cooked in other ways. Stovetop cooking destroys nutrients and vitamins, whereas the pressure cooking method of cooking preserves these very necessary nutrients that our bodies need.

Recipes are placed in different categories, making it easier and faster for you to find for specific meals, or recipes that contain certain ingredients. Each category has a broad spectrum of recipes to cater to the needs and tastes of everyone, from picky eaters to those who want to eat on the run or want pre-prepared food ready in the refrigerator.

Chapter 1: Pressure Cooker Basics

Using a pressure cooker to create delicious meals is not something to shy away from because it is not difficult to use. This is simply a different form of cooking, with some different rules. Once you have mastered the techniques, you are set for life and will never want to go back to traditional stovetop cooking.

Choosing a Pressure Cooker

Choose the most suitable pressure cooker, traditional or electric, that fulfills your specific needs. Choose according to the number of people you regularly cook for. The type of pressure cooker will depend on whether you want to use it for recipes that can easily be prepared in the traditional pressure cooker, or if you want to have a multi-purpose appliance that does the job of several appliances.

Start on the Right Foot

Operating instruction manuals and guidelines are created for a particularly good reason. Avoid endless mistakes and frustration by studying the instructions and familiarize yourself with the workings of your pressure cooker. Modern pressure cookers are amazing kitchen appliances if you take the time to get to know how to use them. Once you have mastered the basics, you can explore the virtually endless variety you can create.

Importance of Liquid Ratio

Many people are unsure about how much liquid to add to pot, as well as the different cooking times, so download a free chart from the internet to assist you. Too little liquid prevents the needed steam from building up in the pot, and if you use too much liquid, your dish will be bland, and sauces will be watery and thin. The general rule of thumb is ½ to 1 cup to enable the cooking process.

Never Overfill Your Pressure Cooker

Cramming in as much as possible will defeat the purpose of a pressure cooker. The pot will struggle to build sufficient pressure to start the pressure cooking process, leading to much longer cooking times. Fitting ingredients in too tightly causes uneven cooking. Spread the ingredients out evenly and fill the pot to ½ or ⅔ capacity maximum.

Herbs and Seasoning

A common mistake people make is adding seasoning and herbs at the beginning of the cooking process and the seasoning loses its potency and herbs are delicate and will lose their flavor when overcooked.

With a pressure cooker, the food inside stays hot for much longer allowing the herbs to infuse the flavor into the food. Make it a rule to always add the herbs and seasonings at the end of the cooking process.

Sauté Aromatic Vegetables

Bell peppers, celery, and onions are the basic aromatic vegetables that most people use. To preserve the full flavor of these vegetables you can sauté them in the pressure cooker with a little oil or liquid of your choice before the actual cooking process.

Thickeners

Thickening stews, soups, and sauces enhance the taste of food. It is important to not add any thickening agent at the start of the cooking process. The pressure cooker needs steam and thick liquids release too little steam. Add thickening agents after the cooking process is completed and let it simmer for a few minutes.

Chapter 2: Advantages and Benefits

Modern pressure cookers available today have changed radically from those available to older generations. The horror stories that people still retell of exploding pressure cookers and lids flying across a room does not apply to modern pressure cookers. The list of benefits of both types of pressure cookers available is impressive and welcome for modern-day cooks with tight schedules and have no time for standing at the stovetop for hours.

Efficient Use of Energy

Pressure cookers remove the need to have several pots bubbling away on separate stovetop burners. One-pot pressure cooker meals bring a significant saving in electricity bills that is most welcome.

Drastic Reduction in Cooking and Prep Time

We all lead busy lives and also want to create appetizing and nutritional food. This often means spending a lot of time preparing a meal when you want a good meal in a hurry. Your pressure cooker is the best kitchen assistant ever. It allows you to present people with an appetizing meal that looks and tastes great even though it took you less time to make.

This is why people are attracted to invest in a pressure cooker as it cooks fast, and you have a meal ready on time, every time.

Nutrients and Flavor

Boiling or steaming food means that you throw away the good with the water. Much of the nutrition is lost with these cooking methods. It is also true that exposing food to very high heat will destroy and deplete the vitamins and nutrients. The cooking process is shortened drastically in a pressure cooker; therefore, nutrients and vitamins are preserved.

Far Less Cleaning Up

Nobody likes cleaning up and washing dishes, especially after an excellent meal. We are all familiar with stacks of dirty dishes, kitchen utensils, and several kitchen appliances waiting to be cleaned. Your pressure cooker eliminates a lot of the usual cleaning as everything goes into one pot. You have a clean stovetop with no open pots simmering away and no food that overcooked and had to be scrubbed off the stovetop. As far as cleaning goes, pressure cookers are an all-round win-win solution for the chefs and the cleaners.

Bacteria

It is proven fact that heat destroys bacteria, that is why medical instruments and equipment are sterilized. Your pressure cooker does that during the high heat and pressure cooking process. Food cooked in a pressure cooker has virtually zero chance of retaining any bacteria.

Versatility

The days of using pressure cookers for stews and soups only have long gone. The modern pressure cooker is the one kitchen appliance that is in use throughout the day. Cook breakfast in the morning, after breakfast you ready the pot for whatever you have on your lunch menu and before you know it, you are prepping your pot for whatever main meal you've decided on.

Besides these uses, the pressure cooker is great for desserts and snacks as well. One-pot can be used multiple times during an average day instead of dirty pots and dishes that would have to be cleaned.

Most modern pressure cookers come with a great list of accessories that makes life so much easier, making your pressure cooker an even bigger asset. These are must-haves for indulging in some serious cooking.

This list is a broad overview of accessories, with some being specifically for an electric pressure cooker and others that can be used in both types of pressure cookers.

- Silicone cupcake liners
- Steamer basket
- Stackable steamer pans
- Glass lid
- Springform cake pan
- Ceramic non-stick inner-pot. This adds convenience as you can start putting together the next batch of cooking while your pot is still busy with the first batch.

- Silicone lid. Instead of transferring food to another container, use the silicone lid and store the food in the refrigerator in the inner pot.
- Sealing rings. This is an inexpensive item worth investing in as sealing rings tend to pick up flavors. If you do a lot of cooking, it is a good idea to have different sealing rings for sweet, savory, and acidic cooking.
- Silicone mini mitts. This is a great accessory as the mitts have ridges and allow for a much better grip when removing the inner pot without any mishaps.
- Yogurt maker

Multi-Functional Kitchen Appliance

The electric pressure cooker is a multitasking work-horse. You have all the versatility of a standard pressure cooker, plus it functions as a crockpot, a steamer, a rice cooker, and a yogurt maker.

It also has a warmer function, as well as a sauté and browning setting. Several electric pressure cooker models also have a special cake maker option. With all these settings and options available, it is easy to find the perfect electric pressure cooker that fulfills all your needs and is within your price range.

No Defrosting

Busy people often forget to take food out of the freezer to defrost before cooking, and this can be extremely annoying. Using a pressure cooker eliminates the need to defrost anything before you start cooking. Simply add frozen ingredients to the pot, and you will have perfectly cooked food at the end of the cooking process.

Safety and Ease of Use

Modern pressure cookers come with built-in safety features that prevent the quite dangerous accidents that occurred with the much older models. All modern pressure cookers go through stringent safety checks to ensure complete safety.

Mechanisms such as the automatic lock prevents the lid from being removed while the pot is under pressure.

Pressure cookers are simple to operate and comes with a detailed instruction manual that guides you through setting up your pressure cooker with tips and advice to ease you into mastering perfect pressure cooking.

Convenience

The electric pressure cooker makes use of the latest technology to give you automation and convenience. You do not have to monitor the cooking process and adjust the heat or change the time settings. Everything is controlled through the built-in microprocessor that is standard for electric pressure cookers. Once you have put the ingredients into your pot, the microprocessor takes care of all the functions and makes necessary adjustments for optimal pressure, heat, and cooking time.

Health Benefits

In previous paragraphs, we have discussed the health benefits gained from better nutrient and vitamin preservation with a pressure cooker. There is another important health benefit for your digestive system as this way of cooking ensures tender food that is much easier absorbed and boosts digestion in comparison with other cooking methods. This is important especially for anyone who has stomach and digestive system health issues and makes mealtimes a pleasure instead of unavoidable necessity.

Cooler Kitchens

Cooking, especially on a hot summer's day can turn your kitchen into a sauna when you have several pots on the stovetop and other kitchen appliances switched on as well, and this is rather unpleasant for the person trying to create a good meal. You eliminate all of the frustration and unpleasant atmosphere in the kitchen by using a pressure cooker. This is a huge bonus point for people living in warmer parts of the country.

High Altitude Cooking

People living at high altitudes are very aware of the differences they have to compensate for in cooking and learn quickly to adjust cooking times. Cooking anything at high altitude simply takes longer, which can be very frustrating when you want to put a good meal on the table and the difference in cooking time increases the higher up you live. Pressure cookers work especially well for high altitudes cooking to save time. An extra benefit of pressure cooking at high altitudes is that the pressure cooker imitates the pressure and moisture that becomes lost at higher elevations. The result is much more tender and appetizing food. Food cooked conventionally at high altitudes increases safety risks because of the lower boiling point of water. Food does not always cook through thoroughly and food-borne bacteria and microorganisms are not always eliminated. Using a pressure cooker at higher altitudes is recommended as it prevents food from being undercooked and tremendously increases food safety.

Chapter 3: Breakfast

The importance of breakfast cannot be stressed enough. We all need to fortify our bodies for the day ahead. It is the same for everyone who lives the vegan lifestyle. The secret is to balance nutrition with taste, otherwise, people will find excuses to skip meals, and this leads to long-term problems we all can easily avoid with the help of a traditional and electric pressure cooker to speedily have a good-tasting and nutritious breakfast on the table.

Stuffed Sweet Potatoes

Prep time: 5 minutes

Cook time: 15 minutes

Total time: 20 minutes (includes pressure release time)

Servings: 1

Ingredients

- 1 sweet potato
- 1 tbsp blueberries
- 1 tbsp maple syrup
- 1 tbsp chopped pecans
- 1 tsp chia seeds
- 1 cup water
- 1 tsp almond butter

Instructions

1. Insert steamer rack into the pot and place sweet potato on top, then add 1 cup of water to the pot.
2. Cook for 15 minutes on high pressure, then depressurize naturally for 10 minutes. Once pressure has dropped, remove the sweet potato onto a plate and remove the skin.
3. Once cooled down, mash the sweet potato gently and drizzle with almond butter and maple syrup and sprinkle the rest of the ingredients on top.

Notes

1. Cook up to 6 sweet potatoes at once and keep the rest in the refrigerator for quick assembly when needed.
2. Add extras to personal taste such as cinnamon, ginger, coconut, and allspice. Extra fruits that go well with sweet potato are stewed apples and prunes.

Pumpkin Oatmeal with Coffee Cake Topping

Prep time: 5 minutes

Cooking time: 5 minutes

Total time: 10 minutes

Servings: 6

Ingredients for pot

- 1 ½ cups steel-cut oats
- 4 ½ cups water
- 1 ½ cups pumpkin puree or used canned 15-oz
- 1 tsp vanilla
- 1 tsp allspice
- 1 tsp cinnamon

Ingredients for topping

- 1 tbsp cinnamon
- ½ cup coconut sugar (or sweetener of your personal taste, or brown sugar)
- ½ cup chopped walnuts or pecans

Instructions

1. Place all the pot ingredients in the pressure cooker. You can use a silicone bowl or steamer pan if you wish. Close and seal the pot and cook for 3 minutes.
2. Mix all the topping ingredients together.
3. After 3 minutes of cooking, turn off the pressure cooker and depressurize naturally.
4. Serve with toppings sprinkled over and the non-dairy milk of your choice.

Notes

- Cook the full bath of oats and store the extra in individual bowls in the refrigerator for later use.
- Do the same with the coffee cake topping. Use what you need immediately and store the rest in an airtight container.

Quinoa Porridge

Prep time: 2 minutes

Cooking time: 2 minutes

Total time: 4 minutes

Servings: 6

Ingredients for pot

- 3 cups unsweetened coconut or almond milk
- 1 cup quinoa

Ingredients for topping

- ½ cup fresh berries of your choice
- ½ cup maple syrup
- 2 tbsp almonds chopped
- 1 tbsp pistachios chopped
- 1 tbsp raisins
- 1 tbsp walnuts chopped

Instructions

1. Rinse quinoa until it runs clear under cold water and place it in the pressure cooker with 3 cups of almond or coconut milk. Depending on the consistency you prefer, you can add up to 5 cups of milk or you can add extra warm milk to the mixture after cooking to thin it to your preferred consistency.
2. Put the quinoa in the pressure cooker on high for 2 minutes and depressurize pot naturally.
3. Put the finished dish on a plate and sprinkle your topping mixture over the quinoa porridge.

Notes

1. This is an extremely versatile porridge and is suitable for breakfast or as a dessert.
2. You can use any plant-based milk for this recipe and add any dry nuts and fruit of your preference.
3. The maple syrup can be exchanged with any other sweetener of your choice or make it sugar-free with Splenda or other non-sugar sweeteners.

Tempeh Breakfast Bowl

This is a layered dish that you assemble inside the pressure cooker pot.

Prep time: 10 minutes

Cooking time: 10 minutes

Total time: 30 minutes

Servings: 4

Ingredients for potato layer

- 28 oz of baby potatoes or new potatoes, chopped into quarters

Ingredients for tempeh layer

- 1 8-oz package tempeh
- 2 tsp soy sauce
- 1 tsp Sriracha sauce or hot sauce of your choice to taste
- 2 tbsp maple syrup
- ¼ cup water

Ingredients for kale layer

- 2 tbsp nutritional yeast
- 1 tbsp water
- 3 cups kale, chopped
- 1 tsp garlic, minced

Ingredients for potato seasoning

- salt and pepper to taste
- 1 tsp smoked paprika

Instructions for potato layer

1. Place vegetable steamer inside the pressure cooker and add potatoes, spreading them evenly and add 1 ½ cups of water.

Instructions for tempeh layer

1. Place tempeh and tempeh ingredients in a short glass pan and toss, covering temple blocks with seasoning. Cover bowl with foil paper and place the covered bowl on top of potatoes in the pot.

Instructions for kale layer

1. Mix all the kale ingredients in a short Pyrex pan and cover with foil paper and place this pan on top of the tempeh pan in the pressure cooker.

Instructions

1. Cook on high pressure for 10 minutes and then depressurize the pot naturally.
2. Toss potatoes in a bowl with the ingredients for the potato seasoning.
3. Serve the dish layered on a plate or in a bowl.

Notes

1. Add other vegetables of your choice and add extra seasoning and herbs you like at the end of the cooking process
2. For firmer textured tempeh, wrap the tempeh blocks in foil paper, then place it into a glass pan.

Buckwheat Porridge

Prep time: 5 minutes

Cooking time: 25 minutes

Total time: 30 minutes

Servings: 4

Ingredients

- 3 cups rice milk
- 1 cup buckwheat groats, raw
- ¼ cup raisins
- 1 banana, sliced or chopped
- ½ tsp vanilla
- 1 tsp ground cinnamon
- chopped nuts of your choice are optional

Instructions

1. Rinse buckwheat before placing it in the pressure cooker and then add all ingredients except the nuts.
2. Close and seal pot and cook for 6 minutes on high pressure and then allow the pot to naturally release pressure before opening.
3. Stir porridge gently before dishing it into individual serving bowls and add extra rice milk if a thinner consistency is preferred.
4. Serve with nuts sprinkled on top as well as any other berries or fruit of your own choice.

Creamy Grits

Prep time: 5 minutes

Cooking time: 13 minutes

Total time: 18 minutes

Servings:4

Ingredients

- 1 tbsp vegetable oil or vegan butter
- 1 cup stone-ground grits (never use instant grits)
- 2 cups soy milk, unsweetened
- 2 ½ cups water
- salt and pepper to taste
- ¼ cup nutritional yeast (optional as this adds a cheesy texture)

Instructions

1. In a standard pressure cooker heat the butter or oil in the pot, and for an electric pressure cooker select the sauté function. Add grits to the pot and stir grits with a wooden spoon or a spatula for 2 minutes.
2. Add soy milk, water, nutritional yeast, and salt and pepper.
3. Seal pot and cook on high pressure for 13 minutes. Allow the natural release of pressure for 10 minutes and then release the remaining pressure manually.
4. Before serving, add extra milk if desired or if there is too much liquid in the pot, sauté for a minute or two to lessen the liquid.
5. Taste and adjust condiments if needed and serve.

Spinach Mushroom Bowl

Prep time: 30 minutes

Cooking time: 30 minutes

Total time: 60 minutes

Servings: 4

Ingredients

- ⅔ cups mushrooms, sliced
- ¼ cup onions, chopped
- 4 cups spinach, fresh
- ¾ silken tofu blended very well
- 6 garlic cloves, finely sliced
- 2 sliced vegan bread toasted and cubed (best to use heels of the bread)
- 1 ½ cup almond or soy milk
- 3 tbsp olive oil
- 2 tbsp basil, fresh
- ½ tsp black pepper
- 1 tsp salt

Instructions

1. Sauté garlic, onions, and mushrooms in oil.
2. Grease a bowl that is suitable to be used in the pressure cooker with oil and place it inside the pot and add the sautéed vegetables to this bowl, then add the bread cubes and spinach.
3. Mix tofu, milk, and salt and pepper in a separate bowl and then add this mixture to the ingredients in the pressure cooker bowl.
4. Cook at high pressure for 30 minutes, then allow natural depressurization.
5. Before serving, add fresh basil leaves and stir.

Chapter 4: Main Meals

The main meal of the day is when everyone starts to unwind after the stress of modern-day living. Your pressure cooker comes in extra handy to get a delicious meal on the table in record time without adding more stress to your day.

Moroccan Chickpea Stew

Prep time: 10 minutes

Cooking time: 22 minutes

Total time: 47 minutes

Servings: 8

Ingredients

- 4 cups vegetable broth, low sodium
- ¼ cup olive oil or vegetable oil of own choice
- 3 (14.5 oz) cans chickpeas (garbanzo beans) drained and rinsed
- 1 (14.5 oz) can diced tomatoes

- 1 yellow onion, chopped in 1-inch cubes
- 1 cup carrots, chopped
- 7 oz baby spinach
- 1 tsp sugar
- 7 garlic cloves, pressed
- ½ tsp black pepper
- ½ tsp salt, kosher or own choice of salt
- 2 tsp sweet paprika
- 1 ½ tsp cumin
- ⅛ tsp cayenne pepper
- 1 tsp cinnamon

Instructions

1. Heat oil in the pressure cooker and when hot add the onions and sauté until onions appear translucent, stirring frequently to prevent burning and sticking to the bottom of the pot. Add garlic and cook for 1 minute.
2. Add cumin, cayenne pepper, cinnamon, and paprika and cook for 1 minute.
3. Stir can of tomatoes with the juices and then add the chickpeas, broth, and carrots and continue to stir.

4. Add sugar, salt and pepper, and stir. Seal pot and cook on full pressure for 7 minutes. When cooking is completed, depressurize naturally for 15 minutes, then manually release the rest of the pressure.
5. Gently stir the stew and taste and add any condiments and herbs you feel will enhance the flavor.
6. Use a fork or potato masher to break up the vegetables if you want a soupier texture or leave whole. Now add the baby spinach, stir gently, and allow it to wilt for a few minutes, then serve.

Lentil Gumbo

Prep time: 5 minutes

Cooking time: 12 minutes

Total time: 27 minutes

Servings: 6

Ingredients

- 1 cup lentils
- 1 tbsp olive oil or vegetable oil of choice
- 3 cups vegetable broth
- optional thickening of 1 to 2 tbsp water mixed with an equal volume of tapioca starch or arrowroot
- garnish with fresh cilantro and sliced jalapeños
- 1 cup cauliflower rice or finely chopped (optional ingredient)
- 1 13-oz can chopped tomatoes, slightly drained only
- 1 cup bell pepper chopped
- 2 celery ribs (1 cup chopped)
- 1 ½ cup onion, chopped
- 2 cups frozen or fresh okra
- 2 tbsp apple cider vinegar

- ½ cup tomato sauce, preferably salt-free
- 1 tsp minced garlic or 2 cloves chopped finely
- ½ to 1 tsp Cajun spice mix (add more to taste)
- ½ tsp cayenne pepper
- ½ tbsp fresh oregano or ½ tsp dried
- 1 tbsp fresh thyme or 1 tsp dried
- salt and pepper to taste

Instructions

1. Sauté bell pepper, celery, onions, and garlic in the pressure pot until fragrant and softened, about 5 minutes, then add spices and sauté for 1 minute more.
2. Place all the remaining ingredients in the pot, except for salt and pepper and mix well.
3. Seal pot and pressure cook for 12 minutes on high and allow the pot to naturally release the pressure; the slow release helps to ensure that the lentils are properly cooked.
4. Add salt and pepper to the pot and the optional thickening mixture if you choose. Keep food warm until ready to serve.
5. Garnish with cilantro, red pepper flakes, and jalapeños and serve.

Notes

1. It is important when cooking lentils to not add salt at the start of the cooking as the texture of the lentils will be ruined by the salt.
2. If you used cauliflower rice, it is not strictly necessary to serve the gumbo over rice, unless it is your preference to add bulk to the dish.

Bologneses Sauce

Prep time: 20 minutes

Cooking time: 30 minutes

Total time: 50 minutes

Servings: 4 to 6

Ingredients

- 1 cup red lentils, pre-soak for 15–20 minutes before cooking
- 7 oz button mushrooms, diced or minced
- 1 large celery rib, chopped finely
- 2 dates roughly chopped
- 10 green or black olives, diced
- 1 large carrot, finely chopped
- 1 onion, chopped finely
- ⅓ cup water
- 2 tbsp olive oil or vegetable oil of your choice
- 1 tbsp balsamic vinegar
- 2 tbsp soy sauce
- 1 vegetable stock cube

1/3c chopped carrots

- 2 cups crushed canned tomatoes or tomato passata
- 1 tbsp tomato sauce (this is optional to add extra tomato flavor)
- 1 tsp white or brown miso (optional)
- ½ tsp salt
- ½ tsp chili flakes
- 3 cloves garlic finely chopped
- 1 tsp paprika

Instructions

1. Pre-soak the lentils, rinse, and set it aside.
2. Use a food processor if possible and dice the mushrooms very finely and set it aside.
3. Add olive oil to the pressure cooker and heat it up. Then add onions, celery, salt, and carrots and sauté for about 7 or 8 minutes while stirring often to prevent sticking.
4. Place the rest of the ingredients in the pot and pressure cook for 12 minutes on high and then allow the pot to release the pressure naturally.
5. Stir the mixture before serving over rice, quinoa, or pasta.

Notes

1. Grated vegan cheese sprinkled on top adds extra flavor and appeal to the dish.
2. Adding some nutritional yeast flakes is always a good option.
3. Garnish with parsley and a few chili flakes to add a special touch to the dish.

Green Curry

Prep time: 10 minutes

Cooking time: 3 minutes

Total time: 30 minutes

Servings: 4

Ingredients for the pot

- ½ cup vegetable stock
- 1 cup cauliflower florets
- 3 medium potatoes, cubed
- ½ red bell pepper, sliced
- 1 cup broccoli florets

Ingredients to add afterward

- ½ cup frozen or canned peas
- ½ cup frozen or canned corn
- 2 tbsp green curry paste
- 1 tsp garlic powder

- 1 tsp onion powder
- 2 cups vegetable stock (add more for a thinner consistency and less to make it thicker)
- 1 cup coconut milk
- salt and pepper to taste

Instructions

1. Place all the pot ingredients in the pressure cooker and pressure cook on high for 3 minutes. After cooking, release the pressure manually, but wait until all pressure has been released before opening the pot.
2. Add all the ingredients from the to add afterward list and stir until the curry paste has dissolved completely.
3. Keep the lid off and put the electric pressure cooker on the soup function and allow the food to heat through completely for about 10 minutes.
4. Taste and add extra salt, pepper, and seasoning of your choice before serving.
5. Serve the curry over rice, pasta, or polenta.

Mac and Cheese with Artichokes

Prep time: 15 minutes

Cooking time: 20 minutes

Total time: 35 minutes

Servings: 4–6

Ingredients for the pasta

- 1 lb egg-free elbow pasta
- 6 cups water
- ½ vegetable stock cube
- 1 onion stock cube
- 2 tbsp olive oil

Ingredients for the sauce

- 1 tbsp olive oil or 1 tsp vegan butter
- ⅔ cups almond milk
- 1 cup vegetable stock
- 1 small onion, finely chopped
- 1 medium potato, cut into small cubes

- 1 cup cashew nuts
- 2 heaped tbsp nutritional yeast flakes
- 1 tsp Dijon mustard or mustard of your choice
- 1 clove garlic, thinly sliced
- 2 tbsp lemon juice
- 1 tsp salt

Ingredients for the final step

- zest of ½ lemon
- ½ tsp pepper
- 2 tbsp parsley, chopped
- 1 9-oz can of marinated artichokes, roughly chopped
- 1 tsp vegan butter

Ingredients for garnish

- deep-fried shallots, no specific amount, of your personal preference
- extra parsley

Instructions

1. Soak cashews in water for 1 hour, rinse, and set it aside.
2. Place all the pasta ingredients into the pressure cooker and mix well.
3. Seal the pot and pressure cook on high for 4 minutes. It should take about 12–15 minutes for the whole process of pressurizing and cooking. After cooking, allow the pot to naturally release pressure for 5 minutes and then release the rest of the pressure manually.
4. Strain out any liquid that remains after cooking and set it aside.
5. While the pasta is cooking in the pressure cooker, prepare the sauce.

Instructions to prepare the first part of the sauce

1. Place a small pot on the stovetop and add olive oil or vegan margarine and bring to medium heat. Add diced potatoes and onions and stir for about 2 minutes.
2. Pour a cup of vegetable stock into the pot and ensure that the potatoes are covered. Boil for 7 minutes, stirring occasionally until potatoes are soft and the mixture has thickened sufficiently.

3. Once cool enough to handle, place mixture into a blender and process for 1 minute. If you want a chunkier consistency, mash the mixture with a fork.

Instructions for the rest of the sauce

1. Place almond milk, nutritional yeast, garlic, mustard, cashews, lemon juice, and salt into a blender and process for about 1 minute until the mixture is smooth.
2. Add the nut cream to the potato and onion mixture and stir until the mixture is fully combined.

Instructions to complete dish

1. Add artichokes, parsley, lemon zest, and pepper to the pasta pot and then pour the sauce into the pasta pot and gently stir and mix until the sauce has blended well with the other ingredients. Taste and add salt and extra seasoning if needed.
2. Serve mac and cheese in a large casserole garnished with parsley and deep-fried shallots.

Mushroom Tetrazzini

Prep time: 10 minutes

Cooking time: 25 minutes

Total time: 35 minutes

Servings: 3

Ingredients

- ¼ cup of toasted breadcrumbs for garnish (toasts in 1 tsp olive oil it is golden brown)
- 8 oz of spaghetti pasta broken in half
- vegan parmesan or nutritional yeast as needed
- 2 tbsp olive oil or vegan butter
- 2 tsp oil
- 2 ¼ cup vegetable broth or water
- ⅓ cup water
- ¼ cup of thick cashew cream (blend ¼ cup of cashews with ¼ cup water until it has a smooth consistency)
- ½ onion chopped
- 8 oz mushrooms
- ¼ cup fresh basil or parsley chopped
- 1 tsp dried parsley or Italian blend herbs

- 1.5 tbsp flour
- ¼ tsp onion powder
- ½ tsp garlic powder
- ¼ to ½ tsp black pepper
- ½ to ¾ tsp salt (adjusted according to whether you use water or vegetable broth)

Instructions

1. Put oil in the pressure cooker and heat well. Add onions, mushrooms, and a pinch of salt and sauté for 3 minutes, stirring often to prevent sticking.
2. Deglaze the pot with 2 tbsp of white wine or water and then continue to sauté for an extra minute. Remove mushrooms from the pot.
3. Add vegan butter to the pot and stir flour into the butter and cook for 1 minute while stirring continuously. Read notes for alternatives.
4. Add salt, herbs, and broth to the pot and bring to a boil. Make sure that the flour does not stick to the bottom of the pot by mixing very thoroughly.
5. Add the broken spaghetti to the pot, ensuring that the paste is fully covered in the liquid. Add ⅓ cup water over noodles for extra liquid covering.

6. Seal the pressure cooker and cook on high pressure for 4 minutes, then carefully do a quick pressure release after 4 minutes.
7. Add cashew cream to the spaghetti and mix. Bring pressure cooker to simmer. In an electric pressure cooker use the sauté option and in a standard pressure cooker let it simmer on the stovetop.
8. Now add half of the mushrooms to the simmering mixture. An optional extra is to add green peas as well.
9. Taste and add salt and seasoning as needed, then mix in the rest of the mushrooms.
10. Remove the spaghetti mixture from the pot and transfer it to a dish and garnish with the toasted breadcrumbs, parsley or basil, and pepper flakes. Lastly, add vegan parmesan.

Notes

1. You can skip making the roux and only use 2 ⅓ cups of water or broth. Then add a few tablespoons of non-dairy cream during the simmering phase to thicken.
2. Make the dish oil free by omitting the butter or oil and skip the flour and sauté in the broth. Add some non-dairy cream at the end for a creamer sauce.

3. Cashew cream keeps fresh for up to 4 days in the refrigerator. Make a large batch and use 1/4 cup for the mushroom tetrazzini and keep the rest to use in other dishes.

Portobello Pot Roast

Prep time: 10 minutes

Cooking time: 30 minutes

Total time: 40 minutes

Servings: 4

Ingredients

- ¼ cup dry red wine
- 2 tsp vegan Worcestershire sauce
- ½ cup vegetable stock
- 2 tbsp olive oil, divided
- 4 large portobellos
- 1 lb baby potatoes
- 1 medium yellow onion, chopped roughly
- 4 large carrots, cut in half into 2-inch pieces
- 2 tbsp tomato paste
- 3 to 4 cloves garlic, minced
- 1 sprig oregano, destemmed
- 1 sprig of rosemary, destemmed
- salt and pepper to taste

Instructions

1. Heat 1 tbsp oil in the pressure cooker.
2. Destem the portobellos and rub well with salt and pepper, then slice them into strips of about ½ inch. Sauté the portobellos for about 3 minutes while stirring. Once the mushrooms are sufficiently browned, remove them and set it aside.
3. Heat 1 tbsp of oil in the pot, add onions and sauté for 3–4 minutes until onions are translucent. Add potatoes, garlic, and carrots and sauté for an extra 2–3 minutes until vegetables have browned slightly.
4. Add portobellos back into the put and pour Worcester sauce, tomato paste, vegetable stock, and red wine into the pot. Add the oregano and rosemary.
5. Before sealing the pot, give the bottom a good scraping to loosen any vegetables that may stick to the bottom. Close the pot and cook for 30 minutes on high pressure.
6. When cooking is done, allow the pot to naturally release the pressure. Once depressurized, remove the lid and allow the portobello pot roast to cool down for about 10 minutes.
7. Serve the dish in 4 individual bowls and share any gravy in the pot between the bowls and serve immediately.

Chapter 5: Lunchtime

Every meal is important, though often people skip lunch as they feel they are simply too busy to make a well-balanced and nutritious lunch. That is no excuse and with a pressure cooker, it is fast and easy to create an appetizing meal.

Pumpkin Walnut Chili

Prep time: 15 minutes

Cooking time: 1 hour

Total time: 1 hour, 15 minutes

Servings: 12 cups (this is a bulk recipe and can easily be adjusted for smaller amounts.)

Ingredients

- 6 cups of broth or water
- 1 cup bulgur
- 1 cup red lentils
- 2–3 chipotle peppers, chopped

- half an onion, minced
- 2 poblano peppers, chopped
- 1 28-oz can fire-roasted tomatoes
- 2 cups walnuts, chopped
- 3 cloves garlic, minced or chopped very finely
- 1 tbsp smoked paprika
- 1 tbsp salt
- 2 tbsp chili powder

Ingredients to add at the end

- 2–3 14-oz cans black beans, drained and rinsed
- 1 14-oz can pumpkin puree

Instructions to start

1. Place all the ingredients in the pot, and for an electric pressure cooker use soup mode and cook for 30 minutes. For a standard pressure cooker, cook on high for 30 minutes.

Instructions to finish

1. Release the steam and add the black beans and pumpkin to the pot and stir. Taste and add extra salt and pepper if needed, as well as any seasoning you prefer. If the consistency is too thick, thin it out by adding broth or water, and let it simmer for 2 minutes.
2. Garnish with cilantro, lime wedges, and avocado.
3. Serve with rice, cornbread, tortilla chips, or your personal favorites.

Notes

1. The amount of black beans to add depends on whether you prefer a strong bean influence in your chili or not, according to personal taste, and you can also use chili beans for extra flavor and heat.
2. Your choice of peppers depends on what flavor you want for your chili. Adding chipotles, jalapeños, and roasted poblanos will give the chili a smoky flavor and add extra heat. Bell peppers add sweetness and mildness to the chili, so adjust your choice of chilis to create the results you want.

3. Excellent for freezing for later use. Make the full batch and portion it into freezer containers and when you defrost it to use, remember to add a little water as the chili tends to thick.

Lentil Sloppy Joes

Prep time: 5 minutes

Cooking time: 25 minutes

Total time: 30 minutes

Servings: 4

Ingredients

- ¾ cup dried green lentils, rinsed and checked for stones
- ¼ cup broth or 1 tsp oil to sauté
- 1–2 tsp vegan Worcestershire sauce and can be substituted with tamari, coconut aminos, or soy sauce
- 1 ¼ cup broth or water
- 2 tsp lemon juice
- 1 cup tomatoes finely chopped, or tomato sauce
- ¼ cup tomato paste
- ½ onion diced
- ½ cup celery chopped
- ½ bell pepper diced
- ½ cup carrots chopped
- 3 garlic cloves, finely chopped
- ¼ tsp black pepper

- ½ tsp salt
- 1 tsp sugar
- ½ tsp smoked paprika
- 1 tbsp chili powder blend, BBQ seasoning, or taco seasoning

Instructions

1. Heat 2 tbsp broth or 1 tsp oil in the pressure pot and add carrots, onion, pepper, garlic, and a pinch of salt and sauté for 3 minutes. Do a deglaze after 2 minutes by adding extra broth.
2. Next add the tomato paste, vegan Worcestershire sauce, chopped tomatoes, lemon juice, and all the spices, and mix well. Check that nothing is stuck to the bottom of the pot.
3. Close and seal the pot and use the chili setting or manual cook on high for 22 minutes, then depressurize naturally.
4. Taste and adjust the flavor by adding salt and condiments as needed.

5. It's important to note that the sauce appears thin and slightly watery directly after cooking and thickens as it cools down. If you add added extra broth or water to the mixture, give it a few minutes to see how much it thickens. If the consistency is too thin, allow the sauce to simmer for an extra few minutes to allow for reduction.
6. Serve on slices of bread, or in buns, in wraps or over baked potatoes with sides of crunchy greens, coleslaw, and onion.

Notes

1. The sloppy Joe mixture can be refrigerated and stays fresh for up to 4 days and can also be frozen for up to 30 days.
2. For flavor variations add any of the following:
    a. smoked paprika
    b. ¼ cup BBQ sauce
    c. ½ tsp mustard of your choice

Burritos

Prep time: 10 minutes

Cooking time: 27 minutes

Total time: 37 minutes

Servings: 8

Ingredients for the filling

- 2–3 tbsp water or olive oil for sautéing
- 2 cups water
- 3 cloves garlic minced
- 1 15-oz can black beans drain off the liquid and rinse beans
- 1 ½ cups corn (canned, frozen, or fresh is suitable)
- 1 ½ cups short grain brown rice uncooked
- 12-oz medium style salsa
- 1 medium red onion chopped
- 1 cup kale finely chopped
- 1 red bell pepper diced
- 2 tsp chili powder
- 1 tsp salt or add more to taste

- 1 tsp ground cumin
- 1 tsp smoked paprika

Ingredients to serve burritos

- 8 10–12-inch flour tortillas
- 1–2 avocados chopped or sliced
- 2–3 cups lettuce chopped

Optional ingredients for serving

- tomatoes chopped
- green or red onions chopped
- jalapeños
- salsa
- vegan sour cream
- vegan cheese shredded

Instructions for burrito filling

1. Add 3 tablespoons of water or olive oil to the pressure cooker and heat. When the pot is ready, add garlic, onion, and red pepper and sauté for 2–3 minutes while stirring.

2. Add the rest of the ingredients for the burrito filling and stir to make sure nothing sticks to the bottom of the pot.
3. Seal pot and pressure cook on high for 24 minutes, then allow the pot to naturally depressurize for about 10 minutes.
4. Stir and taste the mixture and add any spices, herbs, and salt as required and personal preference.
5. Add generous amounts of burrito filling to the flour tortillas, garnish and add optional extras and serve.

Spaghetti with Lentils

Prep time: 10 minutes

Cooking time: 9 minutes

Total time: 19 minutes

Servings: 5

Ingredients

- 1–2 tbsp olive oil
- 2 cups water
- 8 oz spaghetti
- 2 cups green lentils pre-cooked or canned
- ½ onion diced
- 2 cloves garlic minced
- ¾ tsp salt
- 1 25.5-oz jar vegan marinara sauce
- vegan parmesan cheese grated (optional)
- Herbs, spices, and condiments of personal choice

Instructions

1. Add olive oil to pot and heat it up, then add the garlic and onion and sauté for 3 minutes until onions are translucent. Stir to keep vegetables from sticking to the pot.
2. Add cooked lentils, salt, and water. Stir to deglaze the pot.
3. Break spaghetti in half and pour the jar of marinara sauce over the mixture in the pot. Do not stir, but make sure that the noodles are covered in marinara sauce and liquid in the pot.
4. Seal the pot and cook on high pressure for 9 minutes, and to prevent noodles from being over-cooked do a quick pressure release and gently stir the contents of the pot.
5. Sprinkle vegan parmesan cheese over and any extra garnish of your personal choice and serve.

Ramen Bowls

Prep time: 10 minutes

Cooking time: 18 minutes

Total time: 28 minutes

Servings: 2

Ingredients for the pressure cooker

- 4–6 oz uncooked ramen noodles
- 4 cups vegetable stock or broth, preferably low-sodium
- 2 tbsp rice vinegar
- 1 tbsp fresh ginger grated (can substitute ginger in a jar)
- 5 oz shiitake mushrooms sliced
- ¼ cup soy sauce, preferably low-sodium
- 1 cup onions thinly sliced
- 4 garlic cloves minced

Ingredients for suggested toppings

- ¼ cup green onion chopped

- 1–2 tsp toasted sesame seeds
- 2–3 tsp spicy chili sauce
- snap peas or snow peas
- oven-fried or pan-fried tofu
- thinly sliced jalapeños
- ½ cup cooked and shelled edamame
- fresh cilantro
- julienne carrots
- bean sprouts
- baby bok choy
- lime wedges

Instructions

1. Add all the pressure cooker ingredients, except the noodles to the pot. Seal and once pressurized cook on high pressure for 5 minutes. After cooking, do a quick pressure release, making sure to avoid the steam to prevent burn accidents.

2. Add ramen noodles to the pot, and for electric pressure cookers, use the sauté function and for standard pressure cookers, simmer on the stovetop for 3–4 minutes or as per the instructions on the package.
3. Once the ramen noodles are tender, spoon into two large bowls and add any of the suggested toppings and any additional herbs and seasonings to your personal taste.

Mushroom Stroganoff

Prep time: 10 minutes

Cooking time: 20 minutes

Total time: 30 minutes

Servings: 4

Ingredients

- ¼ cup cooking sherry or white wine of choice
- 2 cups vegetable broth
- 3 tbsp olive oil
- 8 oz pasta (penne or rotini)
- 16 oz mushrooms sliced (button, cremini, or shiitake)
- ½ red onion chopped finely
- 3 cloves of garlic chopped roughly
- ½ tsp pepper
- ¾ tsp salt
- 1 tbsp flour
- 2 tbsp mustard (Dijon or whole-grain preferably)

- ½ to ¾ cup vegan sour cream to stir in after cooking

Instructions

1. Heat the oil in the pressure cooker and sauté the mushrooms, garlic, salt and pepper for 7–9 minutes until the mushrooms have released its juices.
2. Add broth, sherry, flour, and mustard to the pot and stir to mix. Then add the pasta and give it another stir.
3. Seal the pot and on high pressure for 3–4 minutes (please see notes), then do a manual quick release. (A good tip is to throw a dish towel over the pot to prevent any burns as the steam releases.)
4. Lastly, stir in the sour cream, and use the electric pressure cooker warm setting or let it simmer on very low heat on the stovetop for 5–10 minutes. This allows the sauce to thicken, but will not result in a stodgy consistency, so you have enough sauce to dip chunks of garlic bread in the sauce.

Notes

1. For extra flavor, a teaspoon of soy sauce can be stirred in before serving.
2. The cooking times for different types of pasta vary, so you may need to adjust the cooking time. Check the time recommended on the pasta package and for example, if the package says 10 minutes cooking time, you halve that plus subtract an extra minute, so the pressure cooking time will be 4 minutes.

Pad Thai Stir Fry-Fry

Prep time: 20 minutes
Cooking time: 20 minutes
Total time: 40 minutes
Servings: 4

Ingredients

- 4 oz whole-wheat spaghetti or use brown rice spaghetti for gluten-free
- 4 cups water
- ¼ cup maple syrup
- 1 tbsp sriracha
- 2 tbsp lime juice
- 5 tbsp soy sauce or use tamari for gluten-free
- 1 large carrot shredded
- 2 cups snow peas
- ½ head red or green cabbage shredded, about 4 cups
- 1 red bell pepper chopped
- 3 green onions chopped, use the tender green and white parts only
- fresh cilantro chopped for garnish
- salted peanuts chopped for garnish
- 1 clove garlic minced
- 1 tsp fresh ginger minced

Instructions

1. Break the spaghetti in half, and to prevent it from sticking together arrange it in a crisscross pattern in the pressure cooker and gently pour the water into the pot without disturbing the noodles.
2. Seal the pot and cook on high pressure for 2 minutes. After cooking, allow the pot to naturally release pressure for 10 minutes and then do a manual release to vent any remaining steam.
3. When fully released, open the pot and drain the noodles using a colander, then rinse the noodles with cold water and set it aside. This step is necessary to halt the cooking process and to remove starch.
4. While the pasta is cooking, use a glass bowl and whisk the lime juice, peanut butter, sriracha, garlic, soy sauce, maple syrup together and set it aside.
5. Spoon the peanut sauce into the pot and add the snow peas, cabbage, pepper, and carrot and stir to coat the vegetables in the peanut sauce. Set an electric pressure cooker to sauté and let a standard pressure cooker simmer on the stovetop for about 5 minutes until vegetables are tender. Test with a fork after 3 minutes to prevent over-cooking.

6. Stir the green onion and noodles into the mixture and simmer until the whole mixture is heated thoroughly.
7. Garnish with peanuts and cilantro and serve immediately while it is hot.
8. Leftovers can be stored in the refrigerator for up to 5 days.

Chapter 6: Snacks

Too often snacks are automatically linked with the word "bad" and that is not what snacks should be. Vegan snacks are wholesome and nutritious and taste great and can be served any time of the day or evening, for totally guilt-free enjoyment.

Cheese Sauce

Prep time: 10 minutes

Cooking time: 15 minutes

Total time: 25 minutes

Servings: 4 cups

Extra kitchen appliances: high-speed blender

Ingredients for the pressure cooker

- ¼ cup raw cashews (2 oz)
- 11 oz russet potatoes diced
- 10 oz sweet potatoes cubed
- 6 oz carrots cut into rounds
- 1 cup water

Ingredients for blender

- ¼ cup almond milk or water
- 1 tbsp white vinegar
- 1.5 tbsp lemon juice
- ½ cup nutritional yeast
- 1.25 tsp salt or to taste
- ¾ tsp smoked paprika
- ¼ tsp turmeric powder
- 1 tsp garlic powder

Instructions for the pressure cooker

1. Place sweet potatoes, cashews, potatoes, carrots, and 1 cup of water in the pressure cooker and cook on high for 5 minutes. Leave the pot to naturally release for 5 minutes and then manually quickly release the rest of the pressure.
2. Allow vegetables to cool down.

Instructions for blender

1. Transfer vegetable mixture to a blender. It is recommended that a high-speed blender is used for this.
2. Add all the ingredients from the list of blender ingredients above and pulse for 30 seconds at a time until the cheese sauce is smooth and creamy.
3. Transfer the cheese sauce to a serving bowl and garnish with fresh herbs of your choice and serve with julienne vegetables and tortilla chips.

Notes

1. To add more flavor to the sauce, add tomato paste, onion powder, and miso paste.
2. For a spicy sauce, add green chilies and cayenne pepper.

Hummus

Prep time: 25 minutes

Cooking time: 35 minutes

Total time: 1 hour

Servings: 12

Extra kitchen appliance: food processor with chopping blades

Ingredients

- 12 cups of water
- ¼ cup extra virgin olive oil
- 1 lb dried garbanzo beans
- ¼ cup tahini
- juice of 1 large lemon
- ⅓ tsp ground cumin
- 2 cloves garlic
- 1 tsp salt
- ⅓ tsp smoked paprika

Instructions

1. Rinse garbanzo beans thoroughly and check for stones. Place beans in the pressure cooker and add 12 cups of water. Seal the pot and cook on high pressure for 35 minutes.
2. Allow the pot to naturally release the pressure. If you are pressed for time, do a natural release for 15 minutes and then a manual quick release.
3. Drain the liquid from the pot into a container for later use and set it aside. It is important to reserve the liquid, so do not discard it. See notes.
4. Transfer 3 cups of the drained garbanzo beans to the food processor while it is still warm and then add the rest of the ingredients, except the olive oil and process the mixture until smooth. Add olive oil to the mixture 1 tablespoon at a time through the food processor tube.
5. Process until the hummus has a creamy, smooth consistency that looks like it has been whipped.
6. Serve garnished with a sprinkling of Za'atar seasoning and smoked paprika and drizzle olive oil over the top.
7. Pair hummus with bread, tortilla chips, pita chips, and julienne vegetables.

Notes

1. The ingredients yield 12 cups of cooked beans. Spoon the rest of the beans into 3 freezer containers and top off each container with ½ cup of the reserved bean liquid and freeze for later use. The sealed containers will also stay fresh stored in the refrigerator for 5 days.
2. It is important to process the beans warm as it gives the hummus a lighter consistency.

Pizza Pull-Apart Bread

Prep time: 10 minutes

Cooking time: 10 minutes

Total time: 20 minutes

Servings: 4–6

Ingredients

- ⅓ cup olive oil
- 1 cup of water to pour into the bottom of the pressure cooker
- 2 tbsp fresh parsley chopped
- 5 oz vegan pepperoni
- 2 cans pizza dough
- 2 cups vegan cheese
- 4 cloves garlic minced
- vegan pizza sauce for dipping

Instructions

1. Cut the pizza dough first into 1-inch strips and then cut the strips into 1 or 2-inch blocks with a knife or pizza cutter.
2. Combine all the ingredients, except the pizza sauce and 1 cup of water in a bowl by using your hands to toss the ingredients.
3. Transfer the mixture to a Bundt pan or a springform pan that will fit inside the pressure cooker.
4. Pour 1 cup of water in the bottom of the pot and insert the Bundt or springform pan into the pressure cooker.
5. Pressure cook on manual or high pressure for 10 minutes and do a manual quick release.
6. Remove the bread pan and transfer bread to a serving platter and serve.

Cajun Trail Mix

Prep time: 10 minutes

Cooking time: 17 minutes

Total time: 27 minutes

Servings: 5 cups

Extra kitchen appliances: oven

Ingredients

- 1 cup raw almonds
- ⅓ cup cashews
- 2–3 tbsp vegan butter
- ½ cup maple syrup
- pinch of ground ginger
- 1 ½ cups raw pecan halves
- 10 oz chickpeas drained
- ¼ cup raw sunflower seeds
- 1 tbsp water (optional)
- pinch of salt
- ½–1 tbsp spicy Cajun seasoning mix

- 6 oz dried mango, regular or spicy to be added afterward (optional)

Instructions

1. Place all the ingredients, except the dried mango, in the pressure cooker and mix well and sauté while stirring until the butter has melted and the chickpeas and nuts are coated with maple syrup and seasoning. If the mixture is too sticky after sautéing, add 1–2 tbsp water and stir.
2. Seal pot and cook on high pressure for 10 minutes and then do a manual quick release.
3. Remove the mixture from the pressure cooker and spread it out evenly on a lined baking sheet and bake at 375 °F for 5–10 minutes. Halfway through the baking time turn the mixture over with a spatula to ensure an evenly baked crunchy mixture. Do not bake the mixture longer than 10 minutes as the nuts burn easily.
4. Remove it from the oven and allow the trail mix to cool down completely and then add the diced mango.

5. Taste the mixture and add any spices and condiments of your own choice to enhance the flavor and then store it in an airtight container.

Notes

1. If you prefer extra crunchy chickpeas, then add some store-bought chickpeas snacks to the trail mix after cooking instead of cooking with canned chickpeas.
2. Make your own Cajun spice blend by combining ¼ to ½ tsp each of the following:
    a. pepper
    b. cayenne pepper
    c. garlic
    d. paprika
    e. onion powder

Hummingbird Muffins

Prep time: 10 minutes

Cooking time: 25 minutes

Inactive time: 10 minutes

Total time: 45 minutes

Servings: 6 muffins

Ingredients

- 6 half pint glass jars, oiled with non-stick spray of your choice
- 1 tbsp chia seeds or flax meal mixed into 3 tbsp of hot water
- ¼ cup coconut oil melted
- 1 ½ cups water to be placed in the bottom of the pressure cooker
- 2 tbsp almond milk or nondairy milk of your choice
- 1 cup all-purpose gluten-free flour blend, preferably without gum as gum may change the texture of the muffins
- ⅓ cup coconut sugar

- ⅓ cup crushed pineapple in juice drained very well (do not use pineapple in syrup)
- ¾ cup mashed banana
- 3 tbsp unsweetened coconut shredded
- 1 ½ tsp vanilla extract or vanilla bean paste
- ¼ cup pecans chopped
- ¾ tsp baking soda
- ⅛ tsp ground nutmeg
- ¼ tsp cinnamon
- ¼ tsp salt

Instructions

1. Oil the jars and set it aside.
2. Pour the water into the bottom of the pot and place a metal trivet inside.
3. Place crushed pineapple, mashed banana, and coconut sugar in a mixing bowl and combine with a spoon or a whisk.
4. In a separate mixing bowl, combine the baking soda, flour, nutmeg, cinnamon, and salt and make a well in the middle of the dry ingredients to enable you to put the wet ingredients into the well.
5. Pour in the wet mixture and combine the two mixtures and then fold in the pecan nuts.

6. Scoop a ⅓ measuring cup of batter into prepared jars and top the jars with ½ tsp of shredded coconut and cover each of the jars with foil before placing it on the trivet inside the pressure cooker.
7. Close the pot and pressurize. Cook on manual high pressure for 25 minutes and then allow natural depressurization for 10 minutes. Release the rest of the pressure manually.
8. Remove jars and allow them to cool down, then remove muffins from the jars and serve.
9. Muffins can be stored in the jars for later use with a lid or covering on each jar.

Chapter 7: Desserts

Dessert is always a treat for everyone and if it not only tastes good but is also healthy and nutritious, that is a huge bonus. Whipping up these desserts in your pressure cooker is fast and convenient, making everyone happy.

Cinnamon Rolls

Prep time: 15 minutes

Cooking time: 30 minutes

Total time: 45 minutes

Servings: 8

Dry ingredients

- 2 tbsp fine or powdered sugar
- 1 cup almond flour
- ½ tsp cinnamon
- 2 tbsp coconut flour
- ¼ tsp salt

- 2 tbsp potato starch
- 1.5 tsp baking powder
- 2 tbsp tapioca starch

Wet ingredients

- a few drops of vanilla essence
- ⅓ cup almond or coconut milk or non-dairy milk of your own choice
- 1 tsp lemon juice
- 1 tbsp oil

Ingredients for filling

- 2.4 tbsp sugar, or a mixture of cane sugar, brown sugar, and coconut sugar
- 1 tsp cinnamon for filling

Ingredients for icing

- ¼ cup powdered sugar
- a few drops of nondairy milk

Instructions

1. Mix all the dry ingredients together in a mixing bowl and add oil and mix again to combine the ingredients.
2. Mix vanilla and lemon juice into the non-dairy milk and set it aside for a few seconds to rest, then add it to the mixing bowl and mix well until it becomes a soft dough. Press the dough gently with hands and if the dough is too dry, add 1–2 tsp of milk. If the dough is sticky, add coconut flour and potato starch 1 teaspoon at a time and press dough each time before adding another teaspoon.
3. Place dough between 2 sheets of parchment paper and press and roughly shape it into a square. Use a rolling pin or your hands to do this until the dough is an even square.
4. Remove the top sheet of parchment paper and brush vegan butter or oil over the dough square. Then mix the sugar and cinnamon and sprinkle evenly across the dough.
5. Roll the dough up slowly from one end, using the parchment paper to help you roll and slowly peel the parchment paper as you keep on rolling the dough.

6. Use dental floss or a strong thread to slice the dough. The dough is soft, and it does not matter if the dough breaks; simply pat it back into place and gently place the rolls into a greased dish suitable to use in the pressure cooker.
7. Add 1.5 cups of water to the pressure cooker and allow the water to heat just below boiling point and place a trivet into the pressure cooker and put the dish containing the cinnamon rolls on top of the trivet.
8. Seal the pot and cook on low pressure for 17 minutes. Alternatively, you can cook on high pressure for 17 minutes with the vent open. Once the cooking time is over, do a manual quick release of the pressure.
9. Remove the dish from the pressure cooker, and allow it to cool down for 5 minutes and then pour the icing over the top. Give the icing a few minutes to settle and then serve.

Notes

1. It is important to use a thin icing as it keeps the cinnamon rolls moist.
2. The rolls are at their best served immediately, but the rolls can be stored in the refrigerator for up to 3 days in a covered container.

3. The almond flour is a major component in the cinnamon rolls as it is a volume flour and replacing it with another type of flour can have a negative impact on the success of the rolls.

Banana Bread

Prep time: 10 minutes

Cooking time: 1 hour 5 minutes

Cooling time: 5 minutes

Total time: 1 hour 15 minutes

Servings: 6

Ingredients

- 1 tbsp flaxseed meal
- 1 1.2 cups all-purpose flour
- ⅓ cup oil
- 3 tbsp water
- 2 ripe bananas
- 1.2 cup sugar
- 1 tsp baking soda
- 1 tsp vanilla extract
- ⅛ tsp salt

Instructions

1. Grease and flour a Bundt pan that fits inside the pressure cooker and set it aside.
2. Whisk the flaxseed meal in a mixing bowl with 3 tablespoons of water until the mixture takes on a gelatinous texture. Set it aside to rest for 5 minutes.
3. Mash bananas and add to the flaxseed mixture. Add the sugar, vanilla, oil, salt and baking powder to the mixture and stir well and then pour the batter into prepared Bundt pan.
4. Place a paper towel over the Bundt pan. After, place a piece of aluminum over the paper towel and secure the towel and aluminum to the rim of the pan.
5. Add 1 cup of water to the pressure cooker and place a trivet into the pressure cooker pot. Place cake pan on the trivet and close and seal the pressure cooker.
6. Pressure cook on manual, high for 50 minutes, and allow the pot to do a natural pressure release for 10 minutes.

7. Remove the cake pan from the pressure cooker and let it cool down for 5 minutes and then place a plate over the cake pan and flip it to transfer the banana bread to the plate.

Notes

1. Sprinkle extra toppings such as chopped walnuts, chocolate chips, candied diced dried fruit in the bottom of the cake pan before adding the batter for extra appeal.

Orange Spice Cake

Prep time: 20 minutes

Cooking time: 35 minutes

Total time: 55 minutes

Servings: 6–8

Wet ingredients

- 3 tbsp melted coconut oil or substitute with applesauce
- ½ cup orange juice and include the pump
- 2 tbsp ground flaxseeds
- ⅓ cup maple syrup or substitute with agave nectar

Dry ingredients

- 1 ¼ cups whole wheat pastry four or substitute with a gluten-free baking mix
- ¼ tsp ground cloves
- 1 ½ tsp ground cinnamon
- ½ tsp baking powder

- ½ tsp baking soda
- 1 tsp ground allspice

Ingredients to mix in

- ½ cup chopped pecans or walnuts
- 2 tbsp orange zest or 1 tsp orange extract
- ¾ cup dried dates diced or dried cranberries

Instructions

1. Oil a 6 or 7-inch Bundt pan that will fit inside the pressure cooker and set the pan aside.
2. Place the 6 ingredients from the dry ingredients list into a mixing bowl. Combine the 4 wet ingredients in a bowl and then add it to the mixing bowl with the dry ingredients. Lastly, fold in the 4 mix-in ingredients into the batter and mix gently.
3. Place a trivet or a steam rack with handles inside the pot and add 1 ½ cups of water. See notes for what to do if you do not have a steamer rack with handles.
4. Pour the cake mixture into the prepared cake pan and cover with foil paper. Set the pan into the steamer rack in the pressure cooker.

5. Close the pot and cook on high for 35 minutes and allow the pot to naturally release the pressure.
6. Once the pot is fully depressurized, move the lid and lift the cake pan out. Allow the cake to fully cool down before cutting as it tends to crumble easily when still warm.

Notes

1. Not all pressure cookers come with a steamer rack with handles. You may find that your cake pan cannot fit into the steamer rack, so you need to make some handles as a safety precaution for handling the extremely hot cake pan.
2. Tear off two pieces of a 3-foot long aluminum and fold each piece over twice. Place the two folded pieces in a cross pattern on your working service and place the cake pan in the center. Bring the aluminum handles up; your cake pan is now cradled and carefully place the cake pan inside the pot by holding the handles.

Apple Crisp

Prep time: 20 minutes

Cooking time: 17 minutes

Total time: 37 minutes

Servings: 4

Apple ingredients

- 2 tsp ground cinnamon
- 3 tbsp almond flour
- 1 tbsp maple syrup
- juice of ½ lemon
- 2 tbsp water
- 3 medium apples cored and chopped (about 3 cups)

Topping ingredients

- 2 tbsp softened coconut oil (optional)
- 2 tbsp softened vegan butter
- ¼ cup brown sugar or coconut sugar

- ¼ tsp ginger
- 2 tsp cinnamon
- ½ cup rolled oats
- ¼ tsp ground cardamom
- ¼ cup almond flour
- ¼ cup chopped pecans

Instructions

1. Grease two glass jars (Wreck or Mason) with cooking spray and set them aside.
2. Combine all the apple ingredients in a mixing bowl, making sure the spices cover all the pieces and set it aside.
3. Turn the pressure cooker on manually or use the sauté function and then toast the oats and pecans for about 4–5 minutes. Stir often to prevent the mixture from burning. Transfer the mixture into a small mixing bowl.
4. Add the rest of the topping ingredients to the toasted ingredients and stir with a wooden spoon or use your hands to mix the ingredients well.
5. Now pour the apple mixture into the two prepared glass jars and divide the liquid evenly between the two jars.

6. Next spoon the topping on top of the apples, ensuring that both jars have an equal amount. Gently press the topping down into the apple mixture with your hands.
7. Place 2–3 cups of water into the pressure cooker and place both jars into the pot.
8. Close the pot and pressure cook for 17 minutes on manual, high pressure and then do a manual quick release.

Notes

1. Do not place the apple crisp mixture directly into your pressure cooker. Always use glass jars because putting the mixture directly into the pot changes the consistency to that of applesauce.
2. This recipe can also be made in a single glass bowl fitted inside the pressure cooker and the mixture can also be divided into three smaller jars.
3. Cooking time can be decreased for apples with more crunch and increased for a softer texture.

Lemon Cheesecake

Prep time: 15 minutes

Cooking time: 15 minutes

Total time: 30 minutes

Servings: 8

Extra kitchen appliances: food processor

Ingredients

- 2 8-oz packages vegan cream cheese
- 2 oz silken tofu
- ½ tbsp vegan margarine
- 1 ½ tbsp toasted almonds
- 12 vanilla wafer biscuits or gingersnaps
- ½ granulated sugar
- ½ natural lemon extract
- 1 tsp vanilla extract
- 1 tbsp fresh lemon juice
- zest of 1 medium lemon
- 2 cups water

Instructions

1. Use non-stick spray to grease a 7-inch springform pan. Cut two 16-inch of foil paper and place the pan in the center of this, then crimp the foil to seal the bottom of the springform pan and set it aside.
2. Put almonds and cookies into a food processor and pulse until nuts are chopped and cookies are crumbled. Add the vegan margarine and pulse to combine the mixture.
3. Place the cookie mixture into the springform pan and press down using your hands.
4. Cube the cream cheese and add it to the food processor with the sugar and process until the mixture is smooth. Now add the tofu, lemon extract, vanilla extract, lemon juice, and lemon zest. Process for 10 seconds, then scrape the sides of the processor bowl and then process for another 10 seconds. Process until the batter is smooth. Transfer the batter to the prepared springform pan and cover the pan with the second piece of foil paper.
5. Pour 2 cups of water into the pressure cooker and place a trivet inside the pot, then place the cake pan on top of the trivet.

6. Close and seal the pressure cooker and cook for 15 minutes on manual high. After cooking, allow the pot to release the pressure naturally.
7. Remove the cake pan from the pressure cooker and set it on a wire cooling rack and remove the foil covering. Check to see if any moisture had formed on top of the cake and dab the cake with a paper towel if necessary. Allow the cast to rest and cool down to room temperature before removing the cake from the pan.

Pumpkin Brownie

Prep time: 5 minutes

Cooking time: 20 minutes

Total time: 25 minutes

Servings: 10

Ingredients

- ⅓ cup oil
- 2 tbsp sugar-free applesauce
- ⅓ cup almond milk
- ⅓ cup pumpkin puree
- ½ cup granulated sugar
- ¾ cup plain flour
- 3 tbsp cocoa powder unsweetened
- 1 tsp baking powder
- 1 tsp pumpkin pie spice
- 1 tsp vanilla extract
- pinch of salt

Instructions

1. Line a 7-inch x 2-inch deep cake tin and spray it with cooking spray and set it aside.
2. Mix the almond milk, oil, applesauce, pumpkin puree, sugar, and vanilla extract together until they are combined. Then add the rest of the ingredients and stir, taking care not to overmix. Pour batter into the prepared cake tin and place foil paper over the top to cover the pan.
3. Pour 1.5 cups water into the pressure cooker and place a trivet into the pot. Place the cake pan with its foil covering on top of the trivet and cover and seal the pressure cooker.
4. Cook on high pressure for 20 minutes and allow the pot to naturally release the pressure for at least 15 minutes.
5. Remove cake pan from the pot and take the foil cover off. Allow the cake to cool for 10 minutes before taking the cake out of the tin. After, place the cake on a wire cooling rack to cool down fully before cutting and serving.

Notes

1. Adjust spices for personal preference and add any favorite spices as well.
2. The pumpkin pie spice can be substituted with cinnamon.
3. Almonds can be substituted by chopped walnuts or chopped nuts of your choice.
4. The pumpkin puree can be swapped for sweet potato puree or butternut squash puree.

Banana Brown Rice Pudding

Prep time: 10 minutes

Cooking time: 12 minutes

Chill time: 1 hour

Total time: 1 hour 22 minutes

Servings: 8

Ingredients

- 2 cups water
- 1 cup brown basmati rice uncooked
- 4 small bananas (5 oz each)
- 2 ⅓ cups unsweetened coconut milk beverage, vanilla flavor
- 2 tbsp agave nectar
- 1 tbsp cornstarch
- ½ tsp cardamom
- 1 tbsp cornstarch
- ¼ cup unsweetened coconut flakes or shredded coconut

Instructions

1. Place the water, coconut milk beverage, brown basmati rice, cinnamon, cardamom, cornstarch, and agave nectar in a bowl suitable for use in a pressure cooker and stir until smooth with a wire whisk and then cover the bowl with foil paper.
2. For electric pressure cookers, press the rice setting and for traditional pressure cookers, cook on high pressure for 12 minutes and then allow the pot to release pressure naturally.
3. Remove the bowl containing rice pudding from the pressure cooker and remove the foil covering. Allow the pudding to chill for about 1 hour.
4. Mash 2 bananas and stir into the rice pudding.
5. To serve, slice the remaining bananas and place them on top of the pudding and sprinkle shredded coconut over the bananas.
6. Additional toppings can be added of your own choice such as vegan granola, finely chopped nuts, any type of fresh berries, and dried fruit like cranberries or raisins.

Chapter 8: Vegetables

Vegetables featured in most vegan dishes, are often combined with grains, tofu and all the things that make vegan meals delicious. Sometimes, we want to prepare good tasting meals or side dishes where the focus is fully on vegetables. Your handy pressure cooker allows you to cook vegetables fast while preserving the nutrition that looks good on the plate and tastes even better.

Collard Greens with Sun-Dried Tomatoes

Prep time: 10 minutes

Cooking time: 15 minutes

Total time: 25 minutes

Servings: 4

Ingredients

- 3 tbsp olive oil
- 1 cup water
- 1 white onion chopped
- 1 bunch of collard greens, hard stems removed and roughly cut
- 1 ⅓ cup sun-dried tomatoes chopped (use the type that is preserved in oil in a jar)
- 3 garlic cloves minced
- ¼ tsp pepper
- ½ tsp salt
- extra sun-dried tomatoes and juice of ½ lemon for garnish

Instructions

1. Put the olive oil and onions into the pressure cooker and sauté for 2–3 minutes until onion is slightly brown and softened. Then add the rest of the ingredients, except the lemon juice, and stir gently to mix the ingredients.
2. Close and seal the pressure cooker and cook on manual high pressure for 5 minutes. Allow for natural depressurization after the cooking process.

3. Drizzle the lemon juice over the food in the pot and stir.
4. Serve warm and garnish with extra sun-dried tomatoes.

Notes

1. Kale can be successfully substituted for collard greens.
2. Although this recipe uses the sun-dried tomatoes that come preserved in oil, this can be exchanged for the dry version of the tomatoes as during the cooking process the dry tomatoes will fully rehydrate.
3. Feel free to add any herbs and spices of your own choice to enhance the flavor, and a good guideline is to choose extra condiments that go well with kale and green beans.

Spiced Mashed Eggplant

Prep time: 5 minutes

Cooking time: 20 minutes

Total time: 25 minutes

Servings: 4

Ingredients

- 2 tsp oil
- ½ cup water
- 1 large eggplant peeled and cut into ½-inch cubes
- ⅓ cup peas
- 1 hot green chili finely chopped (serrano chili)
- 1 large tomato diced
- ¾ cup onion chopped
- 1 inch of fresh ginger finely chopped
- ½ tsp cumin seeds
- 1 tsp turmeric
- 5 cloves of garlic finely chopped or sliced
- ½ tsp smoked paprika
- ½ tsp garam masala
- 1 tsp ground coriander
- ¾ tsp salt

- ⅓ cup cilantro
- ½ tsp liquid smoke added at the end of cooking time

Instructions

1. Switch on the pressure cooker, add oil and allow it to heat up. Put the cumin seeds into the pot and cook for 30 seconds. Then add ginger, green chili, garlic, onion, and a pinch of salt and sauté for 3 minutes. Next, add all the ground spices and mix through.
2. Add tomatoes and cook for 2 minutes and mash or chop larger pieces of tomatoes. Deglaze the pot with a tablespoon of water to loosen anything that may stick to the bottom.
3. As soon as the tomato is tender, add water, salt, and eggplant. Close the lid and pressure cook on high for 9–10 minutes. Allow the pot to depressurize naturally.
4. Mash the eggplant with a potato masher until there are no more big lumps and add ½ liquid smoke. Taste and add salt and other condiments if needed.

5. Let the pot simmer for 3 minutes and stir a few times to prevent anything from sticking. If you prefer a thicker consistency let the pot simmer longer until it thickens enough, then switch pressure cooker off.
6. Lastly, add the cilantro and peas.
7. Serve hot and garnish with pepper flakes, extra cilantro, and a sprinkling of paprika.

Notes

1. To make the dish oil-free, dry roast the cumin seeds in the pot until it releases fragrance. Then add ginger, green chili, onions, and garlic to the pot and stir in a ¼ cup of water or broth and allow it to cook until onions are translucent. Then continue as per the instructions above.
2. To save time, the onion, chili, garlic, and ginger can be processed in a food processor.
3. Add a can of chickpeas to the pot after mashing the eggplant to turn this dish into a full meal.

Potato Carrot Medley

Prep time: 5 minutes

Cook time: 15 minutes

Total time: 20 minutes

Servings: 6

Ingredients

- ½ cup vegetable broth
- 2 tbsp olive oil
- 2 lb carrots roughly chopped
- 4 lb potatoes cut into chunks (Yukon gold or similar)
- 1 white onion, finely diced
- fresh parsley for garnishing
- 1 tsp Italian seasoning
- 1 tsp Vege-Sal Spike natural original seasoning
- 3 garlic cloves finely diced or sliced

Instructions

1. Put oil into the pressure cooker and heat. Add onions and sauté for 5 minutes. Add carrots and sauté for an extra 5 minutes. Then add the remaining ingredients and stir.
2. Close and seal the pressure cooker and cook on manual, high heat for 5 minutes. Then allow the pot to do a natural pressure release for about 10 minutes.
3. Dish out into a bowl and serve garnished with fresh parsley.
4. To add spiciness to the dish, add any hot spices of your choice.

Beets Salad

Prep time: 5 minutes

Cooking time: 20 minutes

Total time: 25 minutes

Servings: 8

Ingredients

- ¼ cup olive oil
- 1 ½ lb beets
- ¼ cup balsamic vinegar
- ¼ tsp salt
- ¼ tsp black pepper
- pinch of fresh or dried herbs to taste (oregano, dill, parsley)

Instructions

1. Wash beets and place them inside the pressure cooker on a trivet or use a steamer basket so that the beets are not submerged. Add 2 cups of water to the bottom of the pressure pot.
2. Close the pressure cooker and pressurize, then cook on high for 15 minutes. After cooking, allow the pot to release pressure naturally. If you are in a hurry, then increase the cooking time to 20 minutes and do a manual quick pressure release.
3. Remove cooked beets from the pressure cooker and rinse under cold water to cool them fast and then rub the skins off the beets with your hands.
4. Cut beets to your preferred size and place them in a serving dish. Drizzle with olive oil and balsamic vinegar. Add salt and pepper and dried or fresh herbs of your choice. Mix to coat beets with condiments and set it aside to marinate for 10 minutes.
5. Leftovers can be stored safely in the refrigerator for up to 1 week.

Notes

1. Herbs that go well with beets are dill, parsley, oregano, and Italian herbs.
2. For a spicier beet salad, add any of the following spices: ginger, ground cardamom, cloves, allspice, coriander, nutmeg, and cinnamon to taste.

Salsa

Prep time: 1 hour

Cooking time: 20 minutes

Total time: 1 hour, 20 minutes

Servings: yield 2 quarts of salsa

Ingredients

- 12 large tomatoes peeled, seeded, cored and chopped
- 1 8-oz can tomato paste
- 1 8-oz can tomato sauce
- 4–6 medium cloves garlic minced
- 2 large green bell peppers washed, seeds and stems removed and chopped
- 2–4 jalapeños washed, seeds and stems removed, and diced (see notes)
- 1 large yellow onion chopped
- 1 tbsp sugar
- 1 tsp cumin
- ½ cup apple cider vinegar
- ¼ cup fresh cilantro chopped
- ½ tsp ground black pepper
- 2 tsp salt

- juice of ½ lime

Instructions

1. Put all the ingredients into the pressure cooker, except the cilantro.
2. Close and seal the pot and cook for 10 minutes on high pressure.
3. After cooking depressurize naturally for 10 minutes and then manually release to depressurize completely.
4. Stir in cilantro and allow the salsa to cool down. Transfer the salsa to airtight containers, preferably glass jars. The fresh salsa can be stored up to 7 days in the fridge.

Notes

1. The salsa can be canned immediately after cooking or can be frozen in airtight freezer containers for later use. If, however, the salsa is going to be canned, it is suggested that canning salt is used in the making of the salsa instead of table salt.

2. The number of different spices to add depends on personal preference and how spicy you want the salsa to be. For extra spiciness, leave some of the seeds in the jalapeños.

Vegetable Stock

Prep time: 30 minutes

Cooking time: 40 minutes

Total time: 1 hour 10 minutes

Servings: makes 2 ½ quarts

Ingredients

- 2 medium onions halved, do not remove skins
- 8 oz mushrooms, cremini or white button
- 2 large carrots (6–8 oz each) cleaned and cut in chunks across
- 2 celery stalks halved and cut across into chunks
- 1 tbsp vegetable oil
- 1 head of garlic halved across
- 2 bay leaves
- 1 tsp whole black peppercorns
- handful of parsley
- 2 tsp kosher salt (optional)

Instructions

1. Add oil to a pressure cooker and let it heat up. Add the onion halves, place cut side down, and leave to cook for 3 minutes until onions turn golden brown. Do not stir the onions.
2. Add mushrooms, celery, garlic, and carrots and toss the vegetables in the pressure cooker and coat them in the oil. Reduce the cooker to medium heat and cook with lid slanted, stirring occasionally until the vegetables are starting to brown and the mushrooms release liquid. This should take about 5–6 minutes.
3. Add peppercorns, parsley, and bay leaves and pour 3 quarts of water into the pressure cooker. Close and seal the pot and cook on high pressure for 40 minutes. Carefully do a manual pressure release.
4. Use a fine-mesh strainer and drain the stock into a large bowl and discard vegetable solids. Add salt if you wish to.
5. Leave it to cool and then refrigerate for up to 4 days.

Notes

1. Vegetables like tomatoes and fennel can be added to the basic ingredients and it will add a sweet flavor to the broth.
2. If the stock will be used in dishes where liquids reduce greatly during cooking, do not add salt to the stock at all.
3. The stock can be frozen for up to 6 months.
4. A great way to build up reserves of the ingredients needed to make this vegetable stock is to save items like the stems of mushrooms that you would normally discard, as well as the ends of vegetables. It is a great saving and it means you have the ingredients for this recipe always on hand.

Cauliflower Tikka Masala

Prep time: 10 minutes

Cooking time: 14 minutes

Total time: 30 minutes

Servings: 4

Ingredients

- 1 tbsp oil or vegan butter
- 1 28-oz can diced tomatoes including the juice
- 1 medium onion, chopped
- 1 small cauliflower head sliced into florets (4 cups)
- 3 garlic cloves minced
- 1 tbsp maple syrup
- 2 tsp dried fenugreek leaves
- 1 tsp turmeric
- ½ cup non-dairy yogurt or cashew cream
- 1 tbsp grated fresh ginger
- ½ tsp ground chili
- 2 tsp garam masala
- ½ tsp salt

- ¼ tsp ground cumin
- optional toppings such as roasted cashews and fresh parsley

Instructions

1. Add oil to the pressure cooker and when oil is hot, add ginger, onion, and garlic. Sauté until onions become soft and caramelized, about 4-5 minutes.
2. Next add garam masala, chili, dried fenugreek leaves, turmeric, cumin, and salt. Keep stirring to prevent anything sticking to the bottom of the pot, for another 2 minutes.
3. Next, add a few tablespoons of water to the pot to loosen the vegetables and scrape the bottom to loosen anything stuck to the pot.
4. Add the maple syrup, cauliflower florets, and crushed tomatoes. Close the pot and pressurize. This will take approximately 10 minutes and then cook on high pressure for 2 minutes. Once the cooking is done, wait for 1 minute and then do a manual quick pressure release.
5. Stir in the non-dairy yogurt and lightly stir the pot to combine the ingredients.

6. Serve hot with rice, or own choice of grains and garnish with roasted cashews and fresh parsley.

Notes

1. If the tomatoes have too little juice, add an extra ½ cup water.
2. Add an extra ½ tsp ground chili if you want to make the dish spicier.

Chapter 9: Soups

Soup is the go-to for most vegan cooks on busy days when you are not in the mood to cook, or just need a bowl of steaming hot, fragrant comfort food that tastes good and looks like you spent hours preparing it. By using a pressure cooker, you take making soup to the next level to create food quickly that appeals to everyone.

Tuscan Pumpkin Soup

Prep time: 15 minutes

Cooking time: 8 minutes plus depressurizing time

Total time: 35 minutes

Servings: 4–6

Extra kitchen appliances: immersion blender

Ingredients

- 1 quart of vegetable stock (see Chapter 7)
- ¾ cup full-fat coconut milk (use canned)
- 2 cups sweet potato peels and diced
- 1 medium yellow onion, diced finely
- 2 15-oz cans pumpkin puree (do not use pumpkin pie filling)
- 1 15-oz can tomato sauce
- ¼ tsp cinnamon
- 2 tbsp maple syrup
- 1 tsp garlic powder
- 1 ½ tsp salt
- optional topping suggestions are fresh rosemary chopped, toasted pumpkin seeds, vegan sour cream, or non-dairy yogurt

Instructions

1. Place the washed and chopped pumpkin, tomato sauce, onion, sweet potato, vegetable stock, maple syrup, cinnamon, salt, and garlic powder inside the pressure cooker and add 6 quarts of vegetable stock.
2. Close the pot and lock the seal. Allow it to come to pressure and cook on high for 8 minutes.

3. After cooking, allow the pot to do a natural pressure release. This is important and a safety precaution as a manual fast release could result in the soup shooting out from the vent.
4. Once the pot is depressurized, add coconut milk and combine the milk with the other ingredients in the pot with an immersion blender until the soup is smooth. If you do not have an immersion blender, use a normal blender and blend the soup mixture in batches, making sure the blender lid is on tightly to prevent the lid from popping off during blending.
5. Taste and add extra salt if needed and serve.
6. See notes for optional herbs and spices to enhance flavor.

Notes

1. These herbs go well with pumpkin and sweet potato so add any of these according to personal taste:
    a. fresh chives, basil, rosemary, and thyme
2. Spices to use for a spicier soup with extra heat:
    a. allspice, crushed red pepper flakes, black pepper, cloves, cumin, and smoked paprika

Lentil Soup

Prep time: 10 minutes

Cooking time: 25 minutes

Total time: 35 minutes

Servings: 6

Ingredients

- 4 cups vegetable broth
- ¼ cup olive oil
- juice from ½ lemon
- 1 cup green or brown lentils
- 3 carrots chopped
- 1 medium onion chopped
- 3 sticks of celery chopped
- 2 cups chopped spinach
- 1 28-oz can diced tomatoes and include the juice
- ½ cup parsley chopped finely
- 4 cloves garlic minced
- ½ tsp dried thyme
- 2 tsp ground cumin
- ½ tsp smoked paprika

- 1 tsp curry powder
- ½ tsp red pepper flakes crushed
- 1 tsp salt

Instructions

1. Pour oil into the pressure cooker and turn on the sauté function or on low heat on the stovetop. Then add carrots, onions, celery, and cook until the vegetables are softened for about 5 minutes.
2. Add the spices and garlic and stir through. Then turn off the pot or remove it from the stovetop burner.
3. Add lentils, broth, tomatoes plus juice and salt and pressurize the pot to high pressure and cook for 15 minutes and turn the pressure pot off and naturally depressurize for 10–15 minutes.
4. Remove 2 cups of soup from the pot and transfer it to a blender and puree, then add it back into the soup pot. Add the chopped spinach and close, but do not seal the pot and let it stand to allow time for the spinach to wilt, which will take about 3 minutes.
5. Lastly, stir chopped parsley and lemon juice in and serve.

Potato and Chickpea Soup

Prep time: 10 minutes

Cooking time: 20 minutes

Total time: 30 minutes

Servings: 3

Ingredients

- ¼ cup broth or water
- 1 cup water
- 1 cup non-dairy milk (cashew, coconut, or almond)
- ¾ cup carrots
- 1 large potato cup into small cubes
- 1 115-oz can of chickpeas drained or 1 ¼ cup cooked chickpeas
- ½ cup vegetables of own choice (broccoli, bell peppers, zucchini, mushrooms)
- ½ tomato diced
- 2 cups spinach chopped
- 3 garlic cloves chopped finely
- ½ tsp onion powder

- 1/8 tsp fennel seeds
- 1/4 tsp garlic powder
- 1/2 tsp oregano
- 1/8–1/4 tsp cinnamon
- 1/2 tsp fresh rosemary or thyme
- 1/2–3/4 tsp salt
- optional garnish ground black pepper and lemon juice

Instructions

1. Pour broth into the pressure cooker and add garlic and onion and sauté until onions are translucent. Scrape the bottom of the pot regularly to prevent sticking and deglaze the pot with a tablespoon of water when necessary.
2. Add in the chopped tomatoes and stir. Then add the herbs and spices and mix in.
3. Put chickpeas, vegetables, water, salt, and non-dairy milk (see notes) and mix.
4. Pressurize the pot and cook for 5 minutes on high, then depressurize naturally.
5. Fold in spinach and allow it to simmer or use sauté function for 1–2 minutes and add cashew cream.

6. Add lemon juice and black pepper to taste. Adjust condiments if needed of your own preference.
7. Serve with garlic bread, crackers, or garlic rolls.

Notes

1. Some non-dairy milk and brands have a tendency to separate when they are cooked under pressure. An alternative to this is to use only water and broth during the cooking process and then add thick cashew cream to the soup at the end.
2. To give the soup a creamier consistency, put a cup of soup into a blender and pulse for 20 seconds, then add the puree back into the soup pot.
3. The chickpeas can be substituted for cooked beans or lentils. If you prefer red lentils, then add ⅓ dried lentils.
4. Soup can also be thickened by adding 2 teaspoons of flour to the non-dairy milk.

Wild Rice and Mushroom Soup

Prep time: 5 minutes

Cooking time: 35 minutes

Total time: 40 minutes

Servings: 4

Ingredients

- 4 cups vegetable broth or water
- 2 tsp oil
- 1 cup pure wild rice or wild rice blend
- ½ onion chopped
- 8 oz mushrooms sliced (a mixture of cremini, shiitake, white, and portobello)
- 1 jalapeño thinly sliced or finely chopped
- ½ cup vegan cream cheese or cashew cream
- ½ cup salsa or replace with tomatoes diced
- 3 finely chopped garlic cloves
- 1 tsp Mrs. Dash seasoning (see notes to make your own)
- ½ tsp dried thyme
- 1 tsp taco seasoning

- ¾ tsp salt or according to own taste
- fresh herbs and pepper flakes or black pepper to garnish

Instructions

1. Heat the pressure cooker pot and add oil. When heated add garlic, mushrooms, onion, jalapeño, and a pinch of salt and sauté for about 3 minutes. Adding 1/4 cup white wine when starting to sauté is optional.
2. Add the herbs, water or broth, rice, spices, herbs, and salsa (see notes for alternatives) and mix well. At this point, you can add in some vegan chicken substitute or rehydrated soy curls as extras. Make sure the pressure cooker is close lit and pressurize the pot.
3. Cook on high pressure for 30–35 minutes, then depressurize naturally before opening the pot.
4. Give the soup a good stir and add cashew cream or vegan cream cheese and set the pot to sauté or let pressure pot simmer on the stovetop. Allow the soup to heat through thoroughly, then taste and adjust herbs and spices if needed. Add water or veggie broth if you prefer a thinner soup.

5. Chopped baby spinach can be added at this stage as an optional extra. Take the pressure pot off the stovetop or turn off electric pressure pot and allow the soup to rest for 1–2 minutes and allow the spinach, if used, to wilt.
6. Garnish with pepper flakes and black pepper to taste and serve with garlic bread or any pull-apart bread of your preference.

Notes

1. To make the soup nut-free, use soy-based cream cheese or non-dairy cream of your choice.
2. For oil-free soup, use 2 tablespoons of broth to sauté instead of oil and remember to deglaze the pot when necessary.
3. Omit taco seasoning and salsa and replace it with parsley, sage, and thyme for a more Italian taste.
4. Make your own seasoning mix that is similar to Mrs. Dash seasoning with the following ingredients that you simply mix together and store in an airtight container:
    a. 1 tsp–1 tbsp mace or nutmeg
    b. 1 ½ tsp cayenne pepper
    c. 1 tbsp savory
    d. 3 tbsp garlic powder
    e. 1 tbsp sage
    f. 1 tbsp onion powder
    g. 1 tbsp thyme
    h. 1 tbsp black pepper

i. 1 tbsp marjoram
j. 1 tbsp basil
k. 1 tbsp parsley
l. zest of 1 small lemon

Vegetable Quinoa Soup

Prep time: 3 minutes

Cooking time: 3 minutes

Total time: 6 minutes

Servings: 4–6

Ingredients

- 6 cups vegetable broth, preferably low-sodium
- 2 ½ tbsp olive oil
- 1 cup quinoa
- 1 ½ cups tomato puree
- ½ cup fresh asparagus or green beans
- 1 cup carrots peeled and chopped
- 1 cup chopped celery
- 3 cups baby spinach
- 1 cup zucchini diced
- 1 cup diced onion
- 1 tbsp Italian seasoning
- salt and ground black pepper to taste
- Optional vegetables that cook soft quickly of own choice can be added

Instructions

1. Heat oil in the pressure cooker and sauté zucchini, onion, asparagus, celery, carrots, and baby spinach until onions are translucent for about 3 minutes and stir regularly to prevent vegetables from sticking in the pot.
2. Add quinoa, tomato puree, salt and pepper, tomato puree, and Italian seasoning.
3. Close the pot and pressurize to high and cook for 3 minutes, then depressurize naturally. Stir the soup and taste. Adjust seasoning to taste and serve garnished with chopped fresh herbs of your choice.

Spicy Carrot Soup

Prep time: 10 minutes

Cooking time: 20 minutes

Total time: 30 minutes

Servings: 4–6

Extra kitchen appliances: blender

Ingredients

- 1 ½ cup vegetable broth
- 1 14-oz can coconut milk
- 1 onion diced
- 8–10 large carrots roughly chopped
- 3 garlic cloves peeled
- 1 tbsp red curry paste
- ¼ cup peanut butter
- salt and pepper to taste
- peanuts and cilantro to garnish

Instructions

1. Add all the ingredients, except garnishing, to the pressure cooker and close and seal the pot.
2. Pressurize and cook for 15 minutes on high pressure. Allow the pressure cooker to naturally release pressure before opening it.
3. Allow the soup to cool for a few minutes and then place it in a blender and pulse until soup is smooth with no lumps. If the consistency is too thick, add extra broth.
4. Taste and adjust seasoning. Top with cilantro and peanuts and serve.

Tomato Soup

Prep time: 10 minutes

Cooking time: 15 minutes

Cooling time: 20 minutes

Total time: 45 minutes

Servings: makes 8 cups of soup

Extra kitchen appliances: immersion blender

Ingredients

- 1 cup water
- 2 tbsp unsalted vegetable broth or water
- 1 cup chopped red bell pepper
- 1 cup diced yellow onions
- 1 28-oz can whole peeled tomatoes
- 1 28-oz can crushed tomatoes
- 3 ½ cups of chopped cauliflower florets
- ½ cup fresh basil, chopped and tightly packed into the cup
- 3 tbsp nutritional yeast
- 3 cloves garlic minced
- 1 tbsp fresh oregano chopped or 1 tsp dried
- ¼ tsp black pepper or to taste
- ½–1 tsp salt or your preference

Instructions

1. Add 2 tablespoons of vegetable broth, garlic, red pepper, and yellow onion to the pressure cooker and sauté until vegetables have softened for about 5 minutes. Stir to prevent vegetables from sticking to the bottom of the pot.
2. Remove pressure cooker from stovetop burner or turn off the electric pressure cooker. Then add the tomatoes, cauliflower florets, water, and oregano. Stir thoroughly until all vegetables are coated and the bottom of the pot has a layer of liquid to prevent burning.
3. Close the pressure cooker and pressurize. Cook on high pressure for 15 minutes and depressurize naturally for 20 minutes before opening the pot. Add fresh basil, black pepper, and nutritional yeast.
4. Use an immersion blender to break up larger chunks of vegetables and tomatoes, but the soup does not have to be blended completely smooth. Alternatively, use a standard blender and blend the soup in batches to the consistency you prefer.
5. Taste and adjust the condiments to taste. It is important to taste before adding salt as many canned tomato products contain extra salt.

Chapter 10: Beans and Grains

Everybody knows that grains and beans can take a very long time to cook and most people don't have the time in their everyday life to do this. Many grab cans and packages from the shop, even when they would much rather cook it from scratch and know exactly what goes into the food they prepare. Your greatest kitchen helper, your traditional or electric pressure cooker is a game-changer that gives you the time to prepare nutritional bean and grain dishes from scratch.

Mushroom Risotto

Prep time: 5 minutes

Cooking time: 30 minutes

Total time: 35 minutes

Servings: 4–6

Extra kitchen appliances: microwave

Ingredients

- 2 vegetable or vegan chicken bouillon cubes
- 4 cups hot water to dissolve bouillon cubes
- 2 tbsp olive oil
- ¾ cup dry white wine
- ¼ cup vegan butter
- ¼ cup soy or cashew cream
- 1 ½ cups risotto rice
- 2 cups dried porcini mushrooms
- 1 lb mixed mushrooms roughly chopped and the stems trimmed
- 1 medium yellow onion diced
- 2 cloves garlic minced
- 1 tbsp white miso paste
- pinch of salt plus extra to taste
- 1 tbsp soy sauce
- pinch ground black pepper plus extra to taste
- a handful of fresh Italian parsley plus extra to garnish
- ¼ cup vegan parmesan plus extra for serving (optional)

Instructions

1. Place dried porcini mushrooms in a microwave-safe dish and add 4 cups of bullion water and microwave for 5 minutes until it simmers.
2. Remove the mushrooms from the bowl and chop roughly, then set mushrooms aside in a bowl. Set the bowl of broth aside as well.
3. Heat the oil and butter in the pressure cooker and add the fresh mixed mushrooms to the pot with a pinch of salt and pepper and sauté for 8–10 minutes and stir regularly to prevent burning, until onions are golden.
4. Add reserved porcini mushrooms, garlic, and onion, and cook for another 3–5 minutes until onions are soft.
5. Next add risotto rice stir constantly while the rice toast (only slightly toasted and not brown) for about 3 minutes.
6. Add miso paste and soy sauce and stir until combined.
7. Pour dry white wine into the pot and stir until the wine starts evaporating for about 2 minutes and then add the reserved broth and make sure the rice is completely submerged.

8. Close and seal the pressure cooker and pressurize and cook on high pressure for 5 minutes. After cooking, do a manual fast pressure release taking care to avoid the hot escaping steam.
9. Open the lid and stir risotto until it is creamy and thick. Lastly, stir in parsley and vegan parmesan.
10. Serve garnished with extra parsley and vegan parmesan.

Refried Beans

Prep time: 15 minutes

Cooking time: 45 minutes

Additional time: 40 minutes

Total time: 1 hour 40 minutes

Servings: 24–30

Extra kitchen appliances: immersion blender

Ingredients

- 4 cups vegetable broth
- 3 tbsp vegetable shortening
- 4 cups water
- 2 lb dried pinto beans cleaned and sorted (about 4-5 cups)
- 1 jalapeño seeded and chopped or thinly sliced
- 1 ½ cup onions diced
- 4–5 cloves garlic chopped roughly
- 1 ½ tsp cumin
- 2 tsp dried oregano
- 1–2 tsp salt
- ½ tsp black pepper

Instructions

1. Place the dried pinto beans in a large mixing bowl and fill the bowl to several inches above the beans and set it aside to soak for 15 minutes.
2. Add the following ingredients to the pressure cooker: vegetable shortening, water, vegetable broth, dried oregano, jalapeño, ground cumin, chopped onion, garlic cloves, and black pepper.
3. Strain the beans through a colander and discard the soaking water, then rinse the beans in fresh water and add them to the pressure cooker. Stir the ingredients in the pot to mix. It does not matter if the vegetable shortening is in lumps, it will melt during the cooking process.
4. Close, seal, and pressurize the pressure cooker. Cook for 45 minutes on high pressure. Once the cooking is completed, allow the pot to naturally release the pressure. This takes roughly 45 minutes. Please do not manually depressurize the pot as the food continues to cook until the steam is fully released.
5. Once the pot is depressurized, open the lid and add salt to taste.
6. Use an immersion blender to break up the beans to the consistency you prefer. Take note that the beans will appear soupy at this stage, but it thickens upon standing and cooling down.

7. Serve as a side dish or a dip with tortilla chips or as a filling for burritos, tacos, and enchiladas.

Spanish rice

Prep time: 5 minutes

Cooking time: 30 minutes

Total time: 35 minutes

Servings: 12

Ingredients

- 4 ½ cups vegetable broth or water
- 2 tbsp olive oil
- 4 cups uncooked brown rice
- 1 yellow onion diced
- 1 red bell pepper diced
- 1 28-oz can diced tomatoes and green chilies
- 1 cup canned peas (optional)
- 1 cup canned corn (optional)
- 4 garlic cloves minced
- ¼ tsp ground cumin
- ½ tsp chili powder (optional)
- 2 tsp salt or more to taste

- pitted, sliced black olives and fresh chopped cilantro for garnish

Instructions

1. Place the oil, onion, red bell peppers, garlic, and rice in the pressure cooker and sauté until fragrant for 1–2 minutes.
2. Add canned tomatoes and chilies, ground cumin, chili powder, salt, and vegetable broth or water and stir.
3. Close, seal, and pressurize the pressure cooker and cook on high pressure for 25 minutes. Allow the pot to release the pressure naturally.
4. Add corn and peas, if using, to the rice in the pot and mix in while fluffing up the rice with a fork.
5. Garnish with fresh cilantro and sliced olives and serve.

Black Bean and Quinoa Salad

Prep time: 15 minutes

Cooking time: 15 minutes

Total time: 30 minutes

Servings: 6

Ingredients

- 2 cups water
- 2 tbsp olive oil
- 1 cup quinoa
- 1 15-oz can black beans, rinsed and the liquid drained off
- 1 red onion diced
- 1 red pepper chopped
- 1 cup corn
- 1 cup edamame
- 2 tbsp cilantro chopped finely
- ½ tsp pepper
- 1 tsp salt
- 1 tbsp chili powder

- 1 tbsp Dijon mustard
- ¼ cup lemon juice

Instructions

1. Put olive oil, quinoa, and water in the pressure cooker in the order as mentioned.
2. Close the pot and pressurize. This takes about 10–15 minutes. Cook on high for 2 minutes and then manually depressurize the pot.
3. Allow the quinoa to cool down in the pot, without the lid on the pot, for about 10 minutes. Mix in the rest of the ingredients and stir.
4. Serve with fresh herbs of your choice as a garnish.
5. This salad stays fresh for up to 5 days in the refrigerator.

Bulgur Salad

Prep time: 5 minutes

Prep time: 5 minutes

Cooking time: 10 minutes

Total time: 15 minutes

Servings: 6

Ingredients

- 1 ½ cups water with salt
- 1 tbsp olive oil
- 1 cup bulgur wheat
- ¼ cup chopped parsley
- 1–3 tomatoes diced
- 2 garlic cloves
- 2 tsp sumac
- 4 tbsp tahini
- 2 tbsp lemon juice
- salt and pepper to taste

Instructions

1. Add 1 ½ cups of salted water to the pressure cooker and bring it to boil without the lid on. Then add bulgur, garlic, and sumac. When the water boils, close the lid and pressurize. Cook on high heat for 10 minutes, and at the end of cooking time allow the pressure to release naturally.
2. In a mixing bowl combine lemon juice, oil, tahini, and garlic. Then stir parsley and chopped tomato into this mixture.
3. Use a fork to fluff up the bulgur and then add the tomato-tahini mixture and stir to mix.
4. Serve with a garnish of your choice.
5. This dish can be served cold or hot.

Bean and Farro Risotto with Kale Pesto

Prep time: 10 minutes

Cooking time: 30 minutes

Total time: 40 minutes

Servings: 4

Extra kitchen appliances: food processor

Ingredients

- 2 tbsp vegan butter
- 2 cups water
- ½ cup dry white wine or broth of your choice
- 1 ½ cup uncooked farro
- 1 15-oz can of white beans drained and rinsed
- ½ cup sun-dried tomatoes (optional)
- 2 cloves garlic minced
- 1 yellow onion diced
- ½ tsp salt
- ⅓ cup kale pesto with extra for serving

Ingredients for kale pesto

- 1 cup fresh basil leaves
- 4 cups torn kale leaves
- 1/4 cup nutritional yeast
- 1/2 cup raw sunflower seeds
- 3 tbsp olive oil
- 1/2 tsp salt
- juice of 1/2 small lemon

Instructions

1. Melt the vegan butter in the pressure cooker. Then add garlic and onion and cook for 2 minutes, while stirring. Add farro a little at a time to the pot while stirring until the farro is coated in the mixture in the pot.

2. When the farro is fully coated, pour the wine in and stir until the liquid has evaporated. Place the white beans, salt, and water into the pot and close the pot and let it built up pressure. This process takes about 10–15 minutes and then cook on high pressure for 10 minutes. After cooking, allow the pot to naturally release pressure for 5 minutes and then do a manual quick release until the pot is depressurized. Stir the risotto and crush some of the beans against the side of the pot with a spoon. Taste the risotto and add salt if needed.
3. Make the kale pesto by adding basil, lemon juice, kale, sunflower seeds, nutritional yeast, and salt to the food processor. Drizzle the olive oil into the processor slowly as the pesto blends. Give the inside of the processor a scrape if the pesto sticks to the side and blend again.
4. Add ⅓ cup of pesto to the risotto, or more if you prefer, and stir until combined.
5. Taste the risotto and add more pesto if needed and then stir in the sun-dried tomatoes.
6. Serve with extra pesto as a topping.
7. Store the leftover pesto in an airtight container in the refrigerator to use with other dishes.

Millet Pilaf

Prep time: 10 minutes

Cooking time: 20 minutes

Total time: 30 minutes

Servings: 5

Ingredients

- 1 ¾ water
- 1 ½ tbsp olive oil
- 1 cup millet
- ½ cup chopped fresh parsley
- zest and juice of 1 lemon
- ¼ cup shelled pistachios chopped roughly
- ¼ cup dried apricots chopped
- salt and pepper to taste

Instructions

1. Add the water and millet to the pressure cooker, close the lid, and pressurize. Cook for 10 minutes on high pressure and then depressurize naturally after the cooking time.
2. Add the rest of the ingredients to the millet and stir.
3. Taste and adjust seasonings to taste.

Conclusion

We have gone through why you need a pressure cooker and all the benefits it gives every busy cook to put great food on the table without having spent hours and hours chopping and stirring. Most people can put food on the table, but that does not mean it tastes good unless they grabbed boxes and cans of the shelves in a shop. Vegans are very particular about what they eat and what goes into their food. Making your pressure cooker your best friend is the wisest step you will ever take to create delicious food very fast that appeals to everyone, young and old, and now you have an assortment of exciting new recipes to show everyone just how good you are.

References

Allyson. (2019). Best Vegetarian Instant Pot Recipes. Retrieved from https://domesticsuperhero.com/best-vegetarian-instant-pot-recipes-pressure-cooker

Braden, S. (n.d.). Gluten-Free Hummingbird Muffins in the Instant Pot. Retrieved from https://glutenfreeeasily.com/gluten-free-instant-pot-hummingbird-muffins

Cooks, C. (2018). Why Are Pressure Cookers Recommended for High Altitude Cooking. Retrieved from https://www.corriecooks.com/pressure-cookers-recommended-high-altitude-cooking

Fields, J. L. (n.d.). Vegan Cooking, Coaching & Consulting. Retrieved from https://jlgoesvegan.com/

Food Editorial Team. (n.d.). 15 Quick and Easy Vegan Meals to Make in Your Pressure Cooker That Are Perfect for All. Retrieved from https://www.onegreenplanet.org/vegan-food/fall-pressure-cooker-recipes/

Gupta. S. (n.d.). Instant Pot Tofu Curry Recipe. Retrieved from https://simplyvegetarian777.com

Hester. K. (n.d.). Plant Based Instant Pot. Retrieved from https://plantbasedinstantpot.com

Huddleston, J. (2019). 14 Vegan Instant Pot Recipes That Make Weeknight Cooking a Breeze. Retrieved from https://www.brit.co/vegan-instant-pot-recipes

Hutchings, C. (2018). 29 Amazing Vegan Instant Pot Recipes. Retrieved from https://www.theedgyveg.com/2018/05/31/30-amazing-vegan-instant-pot-recipes/

Leron, G. (2019). 20+ Easy Vegan Instant Pot Recipes. Retrieved from https://delightfuladventures.com/easy-instant-pot-vegan-recipes

McCauley, T. (n.d.). Vegan Instant Pot Recipes. Retrieved from https://www.thegraciouspantry.com/vegan-instant-pot-recipes

Nussinow, J. (n.d.). Pressure Cooking Basics. Retrieved from https://www.theveggiequeen.com/pressure-cooking

Robin & Felicia. (n.d.). 13 Advantages and Disadvantages of Using a Pressure Cooker. Retrieved from https://kitchensnitches.com/13-advantages-and-disadvantages-of-using-a-pressure-cooker

Seaman, G. (n.d.). Top 6 benefits of Pressure Cooking. Retrieved from https://learn.eartheasy.com/articles/top-6-benefits-of-pressure-cooking

Sina. (2020). 12 Amazing Vegan Salad Recipes. Retrieved from https://veganheaven.org/all-recipes/vegan-salad-recipes/

Thomas. (n.d.). Instant Pot Cauliflower Tikka Masala. Retrieved from https://fullofplants.com/instant-pot-cauliflower-tikka-masala/

Made in the USA
Monee, IL
12 December 2023

48982849R00111